GW01459654

STREATHAM'S 41

An account of the German V-1 offensive against England as it affected Streatham

by

Kenneth Bryant

Senior District Warden
Air Raid Precautions, 1942-45

50th Anniversary Second Edition
compiled by
John Cresswell, Bob Jenner and Colin Crocker

Published by
Streatham Society
142 Harborough Road, London SW16 2XW

"Streatham at War" Series
Titles so far published

Wartime Playtimes
My Travels with E.N.S.A.
Streatham's 41

© Streatham Society 1998

ISBN 0 9504431 5 8

The Streatham Society
is a non-profit-seeking organisation
part of whose policy is
to study and interpret the area
and publish results so that
residents and others may better appreciate
the heritage of Streatham.

A full list of publications is available from the Society

The Streatham Society
142 Harborough Road, London SW16 2XW

Preface to Second Edition
by
John Cresswell

In the final months of World War II Britain was subjected to a bombardment of guided missiles. These V-weapons ("V" for *Vergeltungswaffe* - "retaliation weapon") took two forms. The V-1 (called in this country "flying bomb", "buzz bomb", "pilotless plane (pp)" or "doodlebug") was a cruise missile powered by a ram-jet; and the V-2 was a ballistic liquid-fuelled rocket. Each carried nearly a ton of high explosive and were fired relentlessly at a rate of some hundred a day mainly towards London. At the same time Germany was experiencing the horrors of firestorms meted out by Allied conventional bombers on Dresden, Hamburg and Berlin.

Had the offensive started earlier, the impact of the V-weapons might well have reversed the outcome of the war. The effect on property was widespread and devastating; the effect on the population was terrifying and demoralising. But the Second Front had been opened on 6th June 1944 and as the Allies pushed towards Berlin, the missiles' launching pads were overrun and the bombardment was mercifully brief.

Lying in the target zone of Greater London, Streatham received 41 flying bombs during the summer of 1944, causing nearly a thousand casualties and damage to much of the area. This publication is an attempt to reconstruct the story of those fifty-eight days during which Streatham suffered and the aftermath as the scars of war slowly healed.

"Whether the whole story of the flying-bomb attack as it affected Streatham will ever be written is doubtful. So many things happened so quickly without a complete record being possible - sometimes owing to the tragedy involved - that a full history is impossible," wrote *The Streatham News* in September 1944. An attempt was first made when on 16th March 1945 a small 50-page booklet went on sale called *Streatham's 41*. The publication was compiled by Kenneth Bryant, Senior District Warden. With kind permission of Kenneth Bryant's daughter we reprint the text of his *Streatham's 41*.

The original publication was unique in its first-hand record of the Civil Defence team responsible for dealing with the bombing. This information still makes up the bulk of this new edition although now treated more graphically by relating it to the landscapes upon which the action took place. Because of censorship still in force in 1945, some details had to be omitted in the original book. We have endeavoured to fill these lacunae from contemporary newspaper reports, records, directories and reminiscences to build up the fullest possible picture. It is unfortunate the actual bomb lists for Wandsworth no longer exist for the finer details, but where the blasts affected Lambeth, these sheets have helped complement the picture. Some neighbouring hits have also been added to the map but not elaborated on, although blast inevitably affected our area.

In drawing together these elements as editor of the revised edition of *Streatham's 41* I am deeply indebted to Bob Jenner and Colin Crocker whose original researches are embodied within the text and they must be regarded as joint authors. This volume will be read by many too young to have experienced the war, and I have included an introduction of extra material unashamedly digested from more extended works to place the Streatham episode in context. I thank Lambeth Archives Department, the Wandsworth Local History Library and Greater London Record Office for their facilities; and Mrs Susan Jones for allowing us to use her father's book to illustrate a part of Streatham's history. Many individuals have assisted by giving extra details of the bombing as they experienced the events and we thank them for responding to our appeals. No doubt this publication will prompt a spate of further reminiscences and we would always welcome these.

Fifty years on, it is salutary to remind ourselves and our children of the horrors of war. The Second World War was fought on the streets of Streatham as well as in "some foreign field". We, too, had our heroes - those bravely risking their lives to lessen the number of casualties, and the civilians themselves stalwartly refusing to be beaten. We salute that bravery. It is hoped that present and future generations will never again suffer the terror, the horror, the anxiety of the summer of 1944.

Foreword to the First Edition
by
Sir Ernest Gowers, K.C.B., K.B.E.
(Senior Regional Commissioner for London)

I am honoured by the invitation to write a foreword to this publication. I am the more pleased to do so because I have felt an affectionate affinity with the Civil Defence Services of Streatham ever since that Sunday two years ago when, through the kindness of Mr de Berry, I had the privilege of taking part in a special Civil Defence service at Immanuel Church. There are certain unforgettable things that will always stand out in sharp relief among the jumble of memories that I shall carry with me from my six years as Regional Commissioner. That Sunday morning is one of them.

"Damage and casualties have been reported, some of them fatal." I have often thought, on hearing this bald announcement, that those to whom it meant the loss of their homes and belongings, and perhaps of those dearest of them, deserved to have their sacrifices more worthily and intimately recorded. It was a happy idea to do this for the people of Streatham. It is no longer a secret that they were called upon to bear an exceptionally heavy share of that ordeal in which the indomitable fortitude of the sorely-tried Londoner contributed to the glorious issue of the Second Battle of France.

The Prime Minister once advised us to be *"grim and gay."* He also exhorted us, in the same dark days, so to bear ourselves that if the British Empire and its Commonwealth lasted a thousand years, men might still say: *"This was their finest hour."* Here we can learn how thoroughly the people of Streatham took these injunctions to heart, and how unfaltering were their Civil Defence Services in mitigating their sufferings. Those who come after them must not forget it, and I hope that this record will still be read when the events of last summer will have become a story of

old unhappy far-off things,
and battles long ago.

Preface to First Edition
by
Kenneth Bryant

It is hoped that nothing is included in this book which can hurt or give offence, but there may well be some heart-burning over what has been left out. "Why isn't the splendid first-aid of Smith mentioned?" "...or the hazardous rescue by Brown?" "They haven't said much about our service," and so on. Pity the poor scribe - so many things happen simultaneously at any incident, so much good work is done by so many persons, that it would take corps of reporters and reams of paper to cover only one completely.

I wish to place on record my deep sense of gratitude to the Divisional Office staff. Not only did they successfully contend with a greatly multiplied volume and variety of work and problems, both routine and operational, but the two Streatham mobile canteens were maintained, staffed and supplied by them throughout the period, and turned out promptly at all hours of the day and night.

There are many well-merited tributes to various services included in the text, but primarily the story is told from the warden's view-point, which is only natural as the author is a warden. In my opinion every branch of Civil Defence performed its own allotted function well, but it was the universal spirit of co-operation, real team-work at all levels, which above any other factor gave Streatham during the flying bomb attacks a standard of services second to none.

I am surely speaking for every Officer of the Streatham Services, when I say that the real credit for whatever was achieved belongs to the rank and file - they are fine bodies of men and women with whom it is a proud privilege to be associated.

List of Contents

Kenneth Newell Bryant
Senior District Warden
1942-1945

The Beginnings of the War

The slide towards the Second World War was insidiously slow. Throughout the 1930s opinion in Britain was divided between those who considered it could be avoided and those who saw it as inevitable. But Adolf Hitler's dictatorship of Germany set in motion territorial claims in Austria, Czechoslovakia and Poland that could not be ignored and precipitated the Anglo-French ultimatum.

The 1914-18 War had seen the introduction of aerial warfare. A Zeppelin had even come over Streatham in 1916 dropping bombs. Although relatively rare, the terror from the air remained in the memory. The Spanish Civil War had proved a valuable testing ground for the German bombers, with Guernica as one such unfortunate victim.

Military opinion believed that within a few days of hostilities commencing Hitler's forces would unleash a massive aerial bombardment of high-explosive bombs and poison gas to bring this country to its knees. The people of Britain were as likely to be in the 'front line' as the armed forces fighting abroad. In preparation, means for protecting the civilian population and targets were advocated by the Government, and the Air Raids Precautions Act received Royal Assent in December 1937.

From 1938 almost every home was offered a choice of shelter to protect occupants from bombs. These were mainly two types. The Anderson Shelter was primarily an external form consisting of a pit dug in the back garden covered by a curve of corrugated iron upon which earth was piled. It would not survive a direct hit from a bomb but it proved quite effective protection from neighbouring blasts. The Morrison Shelter was a rigid steel cage constructed inside the house and often doubled as a piece of furniture - a bed or table. It could withstand the weight of a collapsing building. These were to save many lives in the dark years to come.

Public shelters were constructed at several places to serve those caught out of doors. Trenched shelters were dug on Streatham Common. Some public buildings like the cinemas and factories had their own shelters for patrons and workers.

Within minutes of Britain declaring war on Germany on that fateful Sunday, 3rd September 1939, the air-raid sirens sounded in Streatham as elsewhere. It produced both stoicism and panic amongst residents, but it proved a false alarm.

In fact, for many months England was peaceful as the Germans swept through Scandinavia, the Low Countries and France. The precautionary evacuation of children from London and its suburbs to centres scattered throughout the British Isles, the hasty supply of shelters and gas masks, and the elaborate system of Air Raid Precautions seemed unwarranted as the country drifted into the bewildering calm of the "Phoney War". The Streatham & District Chamber of Commerce, in September 1939 complained of the waste of money being spent on A.R.P. "We in Streatham," ran the motion, "view with alarm the large number of persons on paid A.R.P. work who are idling away their time and expending ratepayers' monies, and we would like an immediate assurance that inquiry is being prosecuted with a view of saving ratepayers' money that is now being expended unnecessarily." It was reported that Wandsworth Council (then Streatham's local authority) would have an annual £500,000 bill for A.R.P. The main criticism fell on the paid personnel. However, most were civilian volunteers. Able-bodied men of 18 - 30 years were early conscripted into the Armed Forces unless engaged in vital war industries. The A.R.P. and its supporting groups were formed and run mostly by the older men, with women and youths contributing.

But Hitler had decided to spare the cities: he wanted them intact for his anticipated victory. He preferred instead to eliminate the threat of the R.A.F. defenders against his invasion forces. This offensive - the Battle of Britain - started on 10th July 1940 with the bombing by the Luftwaffe (the German Air Force) of British airfields. It had drained and all but destroyed resistance when enemy bombers unintentionally released their loads on houses on 24th August 1940. Prime Minister Churchill's retaliatory raid on Berlin for this incident precipitated the German Blitzkrieg of bombing on civilian targets (the "Blitz"). For several months, between 7th September 1940 to 16th May 1941, London and other urban areas bore the brunt of almost daily bombing.

Streatham was hardly singled out for special attention by the bombers. The P.B.Cow rubber factory at Streatham Common, supplying rubber dinghies, "Mae West" life jackets and barrage balloon material, was the only obvious local target, as always, were railway lines. But the area shared the terror of random bombing as meted out to suburbia, causing widespread damage, casualties and demoralisation. When the Germans decided to attack Russia on 22nd June 1941, the people of Britain returned to a relative peace again as the Luftwaffe softened up the new battlefront in the east. There were occasional raids on London during the next couple of years, but for the most part it was felt the worst was over.

For the Royal Air Force, the civilian raids were the respite which allowed them to build up their strength. During this conventional bombardment Streatham received 340 high explosive bombs weighing from 50 - 2000kg, plus land mines, oil bombs and some 4500 incendiaries. There were some 120 deaths and much devastation. The men of the A.R.P. had been 'blooded'; they had learnt valuable lessons and awaited further events, although ignorant of the terror yet to come.

Civil Defence in Streatham

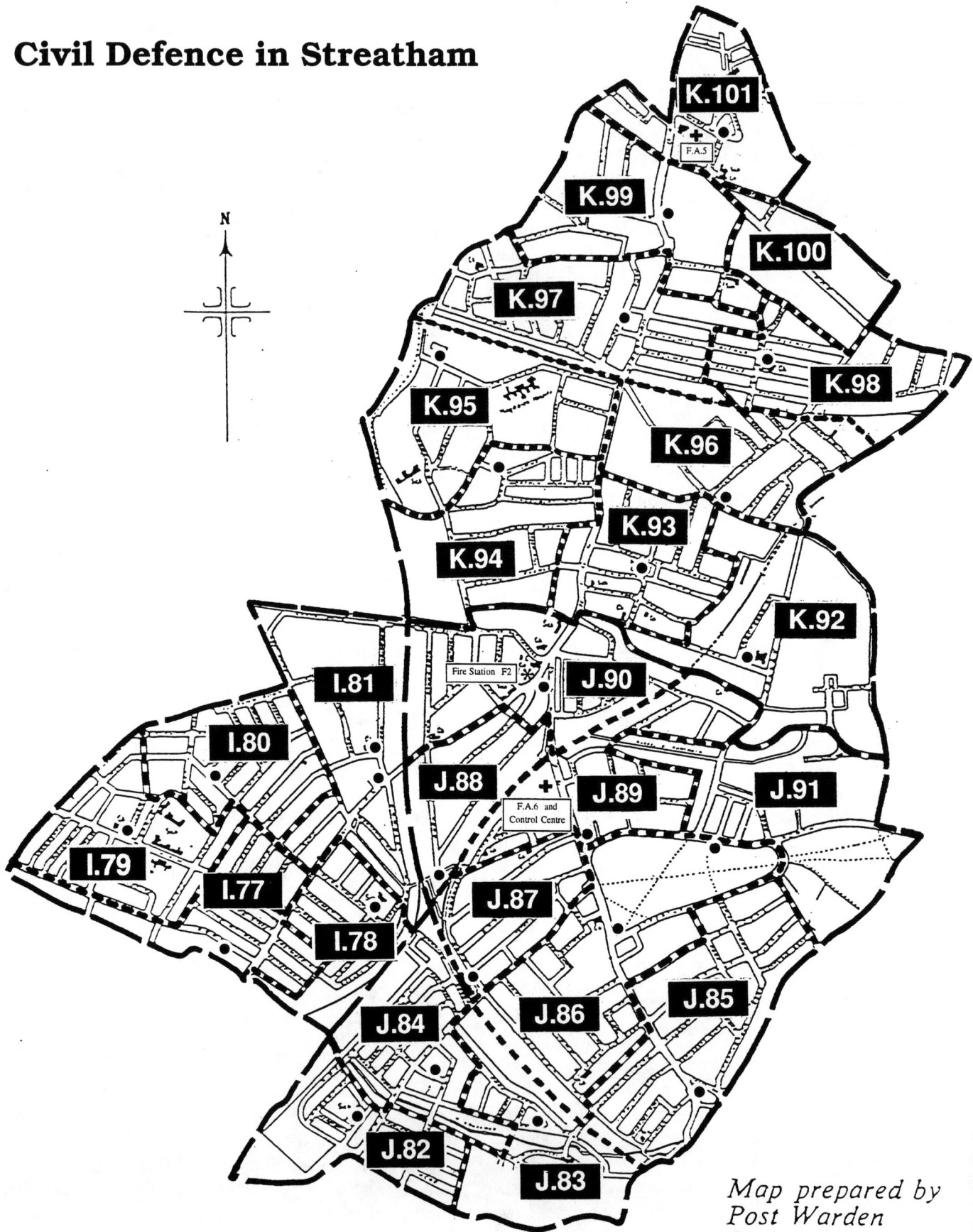

N

K.101

F.A.5

K.99

K.100

K.97

K.98

K.95

K.96

K.93

K.94

K.92

Fire Station F2

I.81

J.90

I.80

J.88

F.A.6 and
Control Centre

J.89

J.91

I.79

I.77

J.87

I.78

J.85

J.84

J.86

J.82

J.83

*Map prepared by
Post Warden
Savoie K—93.*

● A.R.P. Post   + First Aid Post

————— Sector boundary   - - - - - Post boundary

Air Raid Precautions

The Air Raid Precautions had proved the effectiveness of the system in protecting so many lives. A.R.P. - or Civil Defence as it was also called after September 1941 - was organised on a regional basis, there being twelve regions across Britain. London - an area that corresponded roughly with the present Greater London area - was No.5 Civil Defence Region with Headquarters under the Geological Museum in Kensington and managed by London County Council staff. This Region was in turn divided into 9 Groups, each covering several boroughs; 5 within the L.C.C. boundary, and 4 outside.

The Metropolitan Borough of Wandsworth (of which Streatham was a division), together with the Metropolitan Boroughs of Battersea, Lambeth, Camberwell and Southwark, formed No.5 Group of No.5 Region, with L.C.C.- manned Group Control at Nos. 51, 54 and 56 Brixton Hill, SW2.

Authority was delegated from Group to the Air Raid Controller (normally the Chief Executive of each borough) of each component borough in whom the day-to-day running of civil defence affairs was vested. Wandsworth's A.R.P. Committee was set up in 1938. Control was with the Town Clerk at the Town Hall, with a Sub-Control for the eastern half of the borough in the strengthened Rates Office above the public toilets at Tooting Bec. The eastern part of the borough comprised of Tooting and Balham, Streatham and finally Clapham. Each of these divisions had its own control centre, that of Streatham being at Streatham Baths, 384 Streatham High Road. (It was to have been in the basement of a new library planned in Prentis Road but with the onset of war the Baths, although considered not really satisfactory, was retained for the duration.) Streatham Division comprised of three sectors: "I", "J" and "K"; and each sector, in turn, was divided into a series of Posts, designated by the Sector letter and a number (see map opposite). Posts were either purpose-built or converted buildings. The 25 posts of Streatham were manned day and night throughout the war until December 1944. In all there were about a thousand wardens in Streatham, of whom nearly 850 were volunteers.

The linchpin of the Civil Defence was the hierarchy of the Warden Service. A warden was a reporting and controlling agent. His primary duty was to orchestrate the most efficient help required when a situation occurs. Each division was under the control a Senior District Warden, with a District Warden in charge of each sector. Each post was under the charge of a Post

Warden. All these Wardens had Deputies and Welfare Wardens supporting them.

In Streatham, the Senior District Warden during the latter part of the war was Kenneth Newell Bryant, who took over this role on the death of Sidney Sanders in September 1942. Bryant was 39 when he assumed control. He was on the Board of Directors of the South London Motors Limited, 512-522 Streatham High Road. The company was a major supplier of cars but during the war turned its workshops to the manufacture of components for aircraft. It also trained military personnel as mechanics. Despite this contribution to the war effort Kenneth Bryant was given a great deal of freedom to exercise his vital role as Senior District Warden. Gratitude to Raymond Petty, the General Manager of the company, was expressed in a letter from MP David Robertson noting: "how much you are sacrificing in permitting Mr Bryant to devote so much time to the benefit of the community. I feel sure you will be proud that one of your colleagues .. is rendering such signal service to Streatham."

In dealing with air raids, each bomb fall was referred to as an 'incident' - a piece of typical British understatement. At each post at least one warden was trained to be an Incident Officer (I.O.), and the first such qualified warden to reach the site took charge. He covered his tin helmet with a distinguishing blue cover and set up a small temporary command centre - sometimes a fold-up card table. These controlling centres, too, were distinguished either by pale blue flags or, at night, by two blue lamps. Although each warden was assigned a post, bombs were no respecters of arbitrary geographical lines and, provided their own post was not under threat, wardens rushed to any nearby incident to assist. If arriving first to a neighbouring incident, that warden would assume control until a local Incident Officer was appointed. An automatic reinforcement scheme to help neighbouring posts was laid on by the District Wardens a few weeks prior to the V-1 offensive.

The Incident Officer would immediately inform the Borough control at the Town Hall of the exact location of the bomb and an estimate of the damage. At the control each incident was given a unique number and as the incident progressed subsequent messages were logged with reference to that number. Besides the A.R.P. wardens, there were a number of organisations complementing the work. As all these rescue groups gravitated to the site, they took instructions from, and reported back to, the Incident Officer. He held

complete control having authority over every other service attending, including the Police.

Each Post held record cards for every house in its area listing the normal day- and night-time occupants and in which room they sheltered. The public was asked to report any changes to these plans. And if their house was damaged by bombing they were to tell the wardens where they were going before leaving the incident. These lists saved much time by obviating unnecessary searching amongst ruins.

The Warden was able to call upon a number of voluntary and regular services who provided specialised expertise and skills. The **Heavy Rescue Service** was recruited from the building industry. With their knowledge of building construction they could determine the state of damage and make emergency shoring to allow extraction of casualties. Many trapped Streathamites owed their lives to skilled planning by L.C.C. Station Officers Pavey and Strudwick, or their deputies, Elliott and Regan, and the way in which the Rescue Parties executed their plans. Speed in rescue was essential, but so, too, was a sound method of approach, or further collapse way well occur, with fatal consequences for both casualty and rescuer. Once the casualty was reached, a doctor took over direction and the release was carried out according to the condition of the victim.

The **Light Rescue Service** consisted of the stretcher parties - five to a stretcher - who helped bring out the buried casualties from beneath the rubble. Although restricted to a half-dozen parties in each relief, they performed well throughout the area. Once the casualties were removed to hospitals or rest centres, the men assisted with the salvage of furniture and other matters to relieve suffering of the victims.

Medical care was willingly given by local doctors, and first aid was administered by members of the **Red Cross** and **St.John Ambulance Brigade**. Station 188 of the **Auxiliary Ambulance Service** attended all the local V-1 incidents and carried 400 casualties to the hospitals and **first aid posts**. These latter were established at Streatham Baths (**F.A.6**) and the Congregational Church Hall at Streatham Hill (**F.A.5**). They acted as medical filters, treating the less seriously injured, evacuating those needing hospitalisation and capable of travelling to hospitals in the country, and transferring to London hospitals only those who were too injured to travel far. Thus the load was distributed and facilities freed for subsequent emergencies. Welfare workers from the Red Cross visited V-1 casualties every day to ensure their needs were catered for.

The **Women's Voluntary Service** had formed a sub-centre in Streatham on 16th August 1940. Their support to the rescue teams and comfort to the raid victims were to prove invaluable during the various phases of the war. At each incident they opened an Incident Inquiry Point (I.I.P.), either in a nearby hall or a house, where they were besieged with inquiries of all

kinds. Here let it be said that these I.I.P.s were a real godsend and no praise can be too high for the W.V.S. personnel that manned them. There seemed to be an inexhaustible supply of tactful sympathy, practical advice and concrete assistance. It is impossible to name even a fraction of these helpers, but it would certainly be their wish that tribute should be paid to the leaders - Mrs Crisp, Mrs Cronk (until both injured), Mrs Knight, Mrs Larlham, Mrs Bailey, Mrs Irwin, Mrs Kinnersley and Mrs Skinner.

The kitchen at St.Leonard's Hall was put at their disposal and sandwiches and tea were prepared for distribution at rest centres, shelters - and for the incidents. The Streatham W.V.S. were fortunate in having mobile canteens. The first was a trailer, the gift of the American Red Cross, which the W.V.S. Leader, Mrs Churchill-Brown, attached to her own car. Later, more substantial motorised canteens, with serving counters, were obtained. The first was presented to the Civil defence in 1940. Sidney Sanders had opened a fund for the purchase of such a vehicle and it quickly became over-subscribed by the generous response of traders and residents. The second was given by Messrs. P.B.Cow & Co. It was temperamental and hard to start and consequently was given the name "The Brown Cow". They served victims and rescuers alike.

When they had time the ladies attended social evenings and knitted garments for the troops and bomb victims. They produced 8487 garments despite the V-1s. Many knitters, having had their homes blasted, often turned up a few days later smiling and saying: "It's all right, we've saved the knitting."

The **Air Raid Welfare Service** was unique to Streatham. It was initiated by "J" District in May 1941, who arranged that each post had its Welfare Worker with close links with the W.V.S. and its own "Housewives' Service". They were to provide help by opening their homes to bombed-out victims, supplying them with clothing, food and drink.

The regular Fire Service had been augmented by the voluntary Auxiliary Fire Service before the war, but in August 1942 they combined to form the **National Fire Service**. During the offensive we are shortly to describe, fires were fortunately few. With a continual watch, the firemen were often the first on the scene and gave invaluable help to the I.O. During the Blitz, the bombing came mostly at night, but the V-1s fell continuously. Few part-time wardens were available during business hours, and to deal with this situation, a mobile incident team for the whole Division was formed and stood-by adjacent to the N.F.S. headquarters. Column Officer Williams readily agreed to a request that this team should be transported in their vehicles, thus arriving within a few minutes of any bomb falling in Streatham in the day. Later, thanks to the courtesy of the Streatham Hill Theatre, the team was loaned a van which was fitted up to serve as a mobile incident control point.

The **Fire Guards** system which had been set up in September 1943 to cover every street to tackle possible saturation incendiary raids, was also fortunately limited to assisting rescue operations. "J" District, with its 10 posts, boasted some 4000 fire guards. The **Central Firewatching Party** operated from the premises above the Dolcis Shoe Shop at 156/8 Streatham High Road. Some 38 firms in the area provided members from their staff to operate on a rota.

The **Police Force** was overstretched with so many of the younger males applying for the Armed Services, that retired men were re-called. They were supplemented by the part-time "Specials". Although much of the incident operations fell outside their jurisdiction, they gave help where needed, controlled traffic and enforced the law against looters. There was also the need to call upon engineers to attend to the disrupted gas, water and electricity supplies. Such an instance occured when a bomb fell within 50ft of the electricty sub-station in Valley Road (see Bomb 5). Communications, too, were essential in notifying of incidents and for calling up reinforcements.

The **31st London (Streatham) Home Guard** was formed instantly in the wake of Anthony Eden's radio appeal on 14th May 1940. Their role was to provide the last ditch defence should the regular forces be overrun or outflanked. In the latter part of the war it was under the control of Major A.J.Angel, who had seen service at Ypres and Paschendaale. Indeed, the Home Guard were often depicted as the more older veterans of the "last lot". However, a third were youths who went on to join the Forces on reaching 18, having received some elements of military instruction. The Home Guard manned the anti-aircraft rocket battery on Tooting Bec Common. By this stage of the war it was a requirement that about 40% of each battalion was trained in civil defence. Some 50 - 100 men attended the bombings, providing first aid to buildings and mounting anti-looting patrols in wrecked areas.

The V-1s caused many casualties amongst the rescue personnel, and the rescuers often put their duty to others above the needs of their own families and homes. The gratitude owed these people for their courage and devotion should remain on record. A list of A.R.P. officers is given overleaf.

On 30th June 1945 at Mitcham Lane Drill Hall some 800 people - mostly drawn from Civil Defence Services - attended a stand down ceremony at which an album of signatures was presented to Kenneth Bryant ("K.B." as he was affectionately known). The highlight of the evening was a C.D. tableau devised by H.L. Faulkner and F.H.Matthews which depicted all the branches of Civic Defence in their respective war-time roles. It was deemed a fitting and emotional tribute to the bravery and drama of the final months of the war, and, in closing this chapter, it may be appropriate to recall this event with the photograph printed below. With lighting, sound and scenic effects, the tableau concluded with the following lines: "Together we have passed through the fire of tribulation: the fires have branded us into a bond of hearts, into a unity; burning from the ashes of defeat: Victory."

Air Raid Precautions in the Borough of Wandsworth

Mayor and Chairman of Civil Defence Control Committee
Alderman William C. Bonney, J.P., L.C.C.

Town Clerk and A.R.P. Controller: Major R.H.Jerman, M.A., M.C., O.B.E.
Deputy Controllers : L.Morgan and H.G.Thurston.
Officer-in-Charge of Control Room : P.Burr.
Officers-in-Charge of Sub-Control : W.Ebling and G.Herbert.

Chief Warden:	*Casualty Services:*	*L.C.C. Heavy*	*W.V.S. Borough*
Ald. Evan Rees.	Dr F.G.Caley.	*Rescue Service.*	*Organiser:*
		District Rescue Officer:	Mrs Muriel Nutting.
Deputy:	*Light Rescue Service.*	F.Butcher.	
Ald. F.Jordan,	*Commandant:*	*Deputy:*	*Fire Guard Staff Officer:*
(later) H.W.Fray.	J.B.Horton.	S.Wilson.	D.Church.

Shelter Staff Officer : D.J.Fitz-Simons.

STREATHAM DIVISION

The names of some of those who held office in the various Streatham services during the flying bomb attacks are recorded here, but it should be realised that limitations of space alone, not lesser degree of merit, rules out the naming of the entire personnel. Moreover, it would be the special wish of those mentioned, that tribute should be paid to their predecessors who laid the foundations of Streatham's Civil Defence so well and truly.

DIVISIONAL OFFICE

Kenneth Bryant, W.H.Head, Miss J.C.McEwen, A.V.Horrell, G.T.Meekings, Miss J.J.Smith.
C.D. Messengers (Red Cross Cadets) : J.Bull, B.Collins, H.Jarman.

WARDEN SERVICE
DISTRICT WARDENS
Senior District Warden : Kenneth Bryant.

"I" District	T.H.Waight.	*Deputies:*	W.J.Ames, W.J.Dineen.
"J" District:	W.J.Hagger.	*Deputies:*	A.Sheppard, E.J.Tinson.
"K" District:	E.W.Garrett.	*Deputies:*	T.J.Bryant, C.T.Hack.

POST WARDENS AND DEPUTIES

Post I.77	P.Walsh, W.C.Curtis (I.O.), F.A.Randall.
Post I.78	A.J.A.Woods (I.O.), E.H.Long, W.A.H.Usher.
Post I.79	F.G.Greetham (I.O.), F.J.Child, H.J.Miller.
Post I.80:	R.J.Goldworthy (I.O.), F.H.Matthews (I.O.), H.F.Stanford.
Post I.81:	F.G.Archer (I.O.), A.H.Rippon, L.Watts (I.O.).
Post J.82:	W.C.Ratcliffe-Franklin, F.C.Loweth, E.R.Thomas (I.O.).
Post J.83:	F.A.Joslin, R.C.Cook, G.Murrell.
Post J.84:	W.Thompson, F.C.B.Dalton, G.S.Theedam.
Post J.85:	E.G.Edwards, E.J.Brind (I.O.), S.E.Chaplin (I.O.).
Post J.86:	G.F.Byers, J.S.Bell (I.O.), E.G.Osborn.
Post J.87:	P.H.Harrison, C.W.Harrison (I.O.), M.Westfield.
Post J.88:	N.Narracott, W.J.Kingcome (I.O.), J.S.Rogers.
Post J.89:	T.A.Frankford (I.O.), A.M.Bates, C.C.Ford (I.O.).
Post J.90:	W.P.Emuss (I.O.), C.S.Cox, B.W.Oakley.
Post J.91:	P.Ormond-Jones (I.O.), Mrs Caley, G.Robertson.
Post K.92:	A.Brimicombe, W.B.Ashwell, P.M.Chapman.
Post K.93:	P.Savoie, J.Gibb, F.H.Scammell.
Post K.94:	C.O.Randall (I.O.), Mrs Horsey, W.Rosam (I.O.).
Post K.95:	S.L.Hawes, A.Lister-Kaye (I.O.), W.R.Waight (I.O.).
Post K.96:	C.M.Gorringe (I.O.), H.M.Groves (I.O.), H.J.Henderson (I.O.).
Post K.97:	E.G.Lumley, J.Hansen, A.H.Neal (I.O.).
Post K.98:	J.G.Sumner, H.Barker, J.K.Wilkie (I.O.).
Post K.99:	H.E.Dando (I.O.), H.J.Collett, S.Snipper.
Post K.100:	R.Fraser (I.O.), H.J.Grose, F.G.Lean (I.O.).
Post K.101:	D.G.Pumfrett (I.O.), P.T.Bedser (I.O.), A.R.Holmes.

QUALIFIED INCIDENT OFFICERS - WARDENS

H.Abrahams, R.N.Brade, N.Cartlidge, W.C.Foord, H.E.Hill, J.H.Horton, J.S.Ingram, F.J.Jones, F.H.Keightley, G.H.Knight, F.H.Lawman, G.W.Leach, S.G.Letts, W.J.Morley, F.E.Pyne, C.Read, P.H.Smith, H.E.Steele, E.E.Vauzelles, G.C.Watt, W.L.Webb, J.H.Whitfield.

Q.R.C.D. - WARDENS

N.Cartlidge, C.C.Ford, J.Hansen, S.G.Letts, T.A.Taylor

SHELTER WARDENS

"I"	*District Shelter Warden:*	W.J.Dineen.
	Post Shelter Wardens:	W.C.Curtis, W.G.Searle, A.Kelvie, E.Harris.
"J"	*District Shelter Warden:*	Major Sidenham Firth.
	Post Shelter Wardens:	J.W.Ayers, R.Tonkin, W.C.Moore, R.Thiel, Mrs Curtis, A.Thompson, Miss V.B.Skeen, A.Plant, Mrs Smithers.
"K"	*District Shelter Warden:*	C.T.Hack. *Deputy:* A.Robinson.
	Post Shelter Wardens:	W.A.Gray, N.J.Bidlake, T.Gratwick, F.W.West, H.Wright, Miss J.Cave, C.A.Sully.

STREATHAM'S RAID WELFARE SCHEME

Divisional Welfare Officer: Canon D.M.Salmon.

"I"	*District Welfare Warden:*	Miss Milnes.
	Post Welfare Wardens:	Mrs Larkin, Mrs Capel, Mrs Farrants, Mrs Howells, Miss Amor.
"J"	*District Welfare Warden:*	H.L.Faulkner.
	Post Welfare Wardens:	A.E.Vose, Mrs Smith, J.Lawrence, Mrs Edwards, Mrs Osborn (*Deputy District*), Mrs Jarvis, Miss L.Narracott, J.J.F.Johnson, A.Plant, Mrs Smith.
"K"	*District Welfare Warden:*	E.Belham.
	Post Welfare Wardens:	C.H.Masters, Mrs Crosskey, Mrs Ramsden, Mrs Bingham, Mrs Trenerry, Mrs Barker, M.W.Hunt (*Deputy District*), Miss E.Wells, Mrs Perryman, A.Lockwood.

Also District and Post Leaders of the W.V.S.

L.C.C. HEAVY RESCUE SERVICE

Station Rescue Officers:	D.J.Pavey, G.A.Strudwick.
Station Rescue Foremen:	G.Elliott, G.Regan.
Party Leaders:	E.Cheall, A.Clark, G.Parkinson, H.Bransgrove, E.Steel, S.Salter, J.McFarlane, F.Stapleton.

LIGHT RESCUE SERVICE

Officer-in-Charge:	A.W.Wilson.
Station Officers:	E.Barnard, G.Russell-Owen.
Sergeants:	E.H.Bish, H.W.Brown, P.H.G.Matthews, L.S.Viney, R.G.Parker, J.W.Jelly, D.C.West, A.E.Chamberlain.
Corporals:	H.W.Ball, H.W.Bird, W.A.Hand, A.L.Chamberlain, J.F.Hennessy, L.C.Quinn, A.C.Stanley, E.Hall, W.F.Bouter, A.T.Fuggle, J.C.Hicken, G.H.Overall, F.W.Weston, G.H.Winter.

NATIONAL FIRE SERVICE

N.F.S. Officers who attended incidents in Streatham include:

Divisional Officers:	Baker, Denyer.
Column Officers:	Andrews, Williams.
Company Officers:	Annison, Boxall, Langford, Sharr, Skinner.
Section Leaders:	Blatchford, Colbourn, Dibbs, Dunk, Everest, Fitzgerald, French, Guy, Harris, Logan, Scales, Spicer, Sturges, Ward, Waters.

FIRE GUARD

Divisional Fire Guard: Councillor F.H.Campbell.
H.E.Wates (*Training officer*), W.H.Cantler, Mrs D.M.Chubb, Mrs L.G.Davenport, A.Jackson, Mrs M.R.Ross, J.W.Thursby, J.Valles, H.V.Walker.

"I"	*Head Fire Guard:*	C.Turner.
	Senior Fire Guards:	J.M.Irwin, G.Trodd, T.Watkins, E.F.Sainsbury, S.C.Lawrence.
"J"	*Head Fire Guard:*	S.A.Cotton.
	Senior Fire Guards:	C.H.Burchett, M.Torch, J.B.Noel, C.A.Wakeling, W.W.Charman, H.Carter, T.A.Walsh, H.S.Dove, A.E.Henderson, H.K.Taylor.
"K"	*Head Fire Guard:*	H.L.Hughes.
	Senior Fire Guards:	K.M.Currie, B.J.Lynes, S.Levy, A.E.Smart, W.C.Wyatt, E.G.Allard, A.L.Middleton, S.C.Colman, R.H.Egleton.

FIRST AID POSTS Nos. 5 & 6

Sister-in-Charge: Mrs D.Rogers.

Deputies	(*No.5*):	Miss M.E.Langley.
	(*No.6*):	Miss D.Barker.
Medical Officers	(*No.5*):	Dr Stewart-Hunter.
	(*No.6*):	Dr G.R.Hull.

WOMEN'S VOLUNTARY SERVICE

Sub-Centre Organiser: Mrs Crisp (until injured), then Mrs Knight.
Mrs Cronk, Mrs Larlham, Mrs Silkstone, Mrs Thornley, Miss V.Wright.

"I"	*District Leader:*	Mrs Irwin.
	Post Leaders:	Mrs Gentleman, Mrs Thurgood, Mrs Manley, Mrs Fisher, Mrs Etches.
"J"	*District Leader:*	Mrs Bailey.
	Post Leaders:	Mrs Lodge, Mrs Clarke, Mrs Thompson, Mrs Randall, Mrs Jarvis, Mrs Frost, Mrs Dare, Mrs Lindenboom, Miss Kidby, Miss Maynard.
"K"	*District Leaders:*	Mrs Kinnersley, Mrs Skinner.
	Post Leaders:	Mrs Horrell, Mrs Savoie, Mrs O'Dwyer, Mrs McDermott, Mrs Webb, Mrs Levy, Mrs Morgan, Mrs Cass, Mrs Warner, Mrs Goodridge.

Amongst the many others who helped, great assistance was received from:

London Auxiliary Ambulance Service
Borough Engineer's Department
The Police (Streatham & Tooting Divisions)
The Home Guard (30th and 31st London)

Range
propeller

Magnetic
compass
and gyros

Warhead

Fuel tank

Compressed air
bottles

Ramjet

Exhaust
nozzle

Rudder

Elevator

Autopilot and
Pneumatic servos
controlling
rudder and
elevators

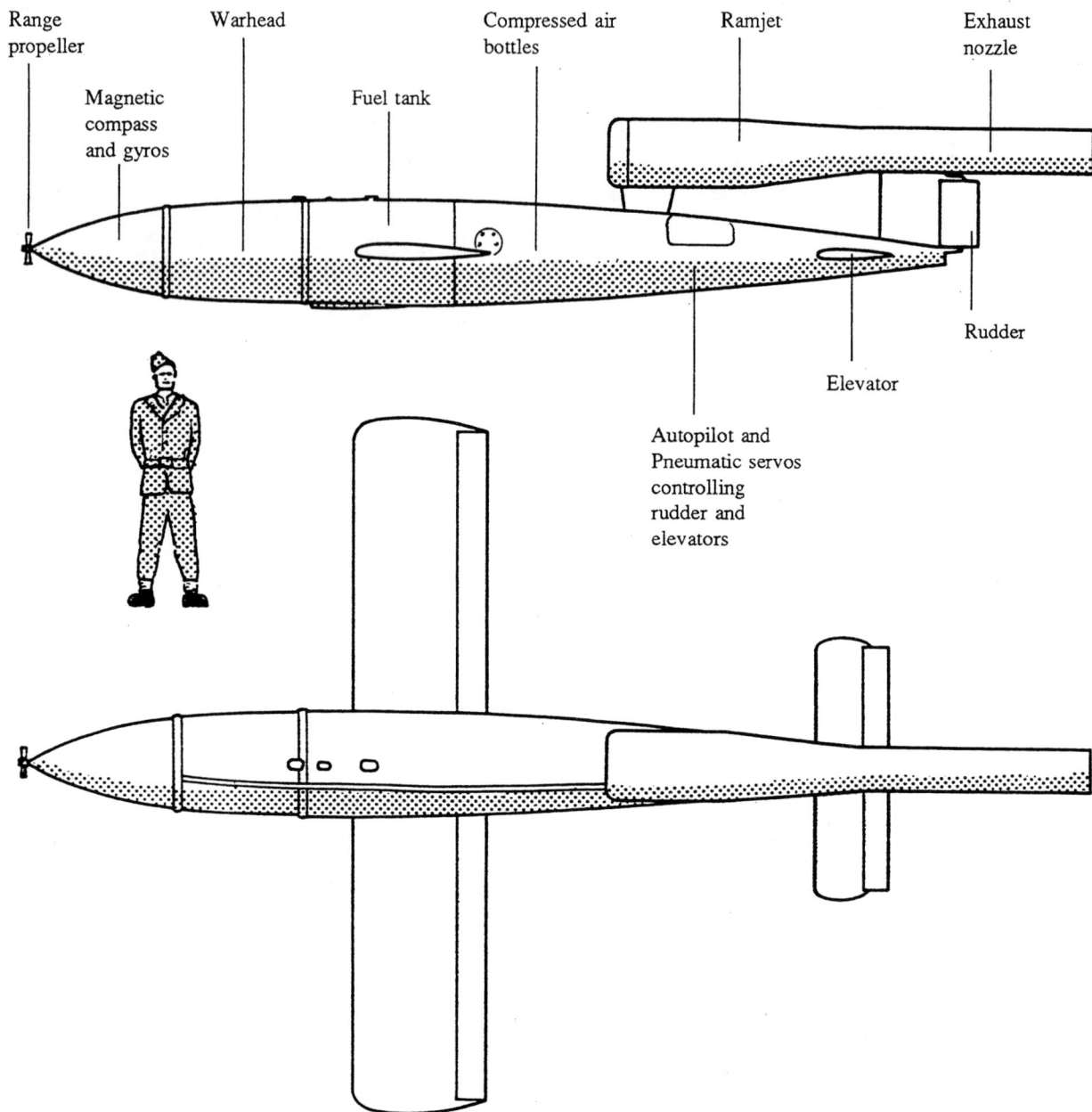

Schematic Diagram of Ramjet Operation

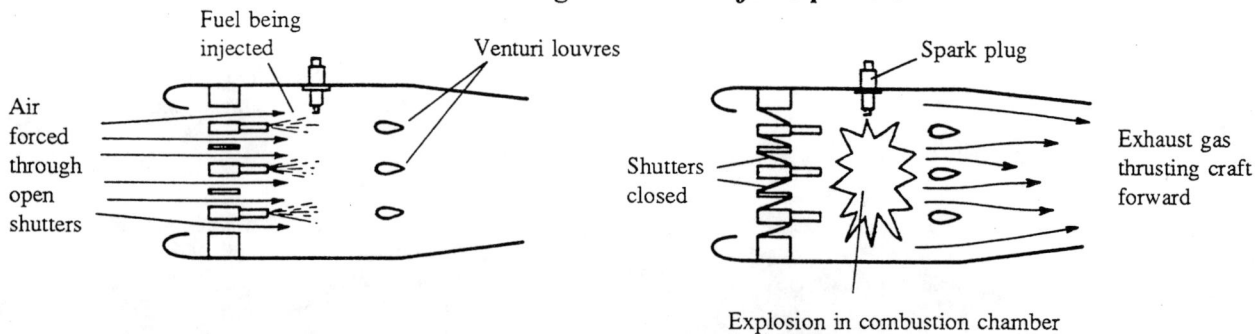

Fuel being
injected

Venturi louvres

Spark plug

Air
forced
through
open
shutters

Shutters
closed

Exhaust gas
thrusting craft
forward

Explosion in combustion chamber

Stage A

With motion of launch, air is forced
into combustion chamber through
spring-operated shutters. At the same
time, fuel is injected into chamber.

Stage B

The shutters closed, the air/fuel mixture
is exploded by the spark plug and the
expanding gases are ejected through the
rear, speeding up through the venturi.

The German Vengeance Weapons

When Adolf Hitler became Chancellor of the Third Reich in 1933, he promised a revival of German supremacy, in technology as in other spheres. The armed forces received encouragement to develop novel weapons. The Army had been investigating the possibilities of cheap missiles based on liquid propellant since 1929. Wernher von Braun, whose student vision of space travel had explored the new techniques, was employed at Kummersdorf, and by 1934 had developed a 1.4 metre long rocket using alcohol and liquid oxygen. Termed Aggregat 1 (A1), it established the basis for a new breed of weaponry - guided missiles. The Army specified their requirements of a transportable rocket with a 300km range carrying a 1 ton warhead.

By 1937 the small fishing village of Peenemünde on the Baltic island of Usedom was being developed as a research station. For several years it was to be the main centre for the testing of new weapons.

Meanwhile, the German Air Force (the Luftwaffe) sought to devise its own missile. The origins of this weapon also goes back to the early 1930s, although the motor design was conceived in France in 1907. Prior to the outbreak of World War II both Paul Schmidt, a Munich engineer, and the Argus Motorwerk were perfecting the engine. Their combined efforts produced the Argus-Schmidtröhr, As 109-014, which was tested on a Gotha biplane in April 1941. It was an air-breathing ram-jet. 3.35m long, it was basically a tube. The motive power could only be activated when given a powerful forward thrust. This forced air through a bank of one-way spring valves into a chamber, where it was mixed with injected butane. The air-gas mixture was ignited with a single spark plug and with the valves closed, the expanded gas was ejected through the rear nozzle. Repeated some 40-45 times a second, the engine could propel an aircraft to a speed of around 400 mph.

At the same time the missile was being developed by Robert Lusser at the Gerhard Fieseler Werke G.m.b.H.: the Fi103. Because of its intended function it was also known as FZG 76 (*Flakzeitlgerat* - Anti Aircraft Aiming Device). It was a smallish cruciform craft with a torpedo-shaped fuselage and straight wings. It measured 7.9m (26ft) overall with a span of 5.3m (17ft 6in). It weighed 2,180kg (4800lb) fully armed. The body was constructed almost entirely of welded steel sheet. It had six compartments. In the forward bay was the magnetic compass and gyros providing the simple guidance mechanism, and on the nose itself was a small propeller - an anemometer - which was a crude range-setter, and after a specified number of turns it triggered a tilting of the flaps to make the machine dive at the end of its intended flight. Behind this was the 850kg warhead of Amatol - a mixture of trinitrotoluene (TNT) and ammonium nitrate. The next

compartment held the 150 gallons of fuel. Behind this were a couple of light-gauge steel spheres, reinforced by steel bands which contained the compressed air to supply the autopilot and various relays and servos. These latter controlling mechanisms were placed in the tail bays near the rudders and elevators which they controlled. The As014 motor was mounted above and at the rear of the fuselage. To provide the initial thrust the FZG 76 was launched from a ramp some 55m (180ft) long, inclined at an angle of 6°. The ramps were built of concrete along the length of which ran a gas-driven piston which catapulted the missile off at a speed of nearly 200 mph.

It was the simplicity of the motor and its cheapness (around £600; cf. a British torpedo costing £2000) that made possible the concept of the FZG 76 as an expendable missile. By 1940 the German Army had produced its first large rocket - the A4 - but this was at enormous expense.

Hitler having conquered most of Europe so quickly with conventional weapons felt less inclined to continue the research at Peenemünde, believing the rockets had come too late. By the end of 1941, however, he had cause to re-think the situation: Britain still remained undefeated, the war with Russia was stretching resources, and the United States had joined the war with the Allies.

By 1942 the first A4 rockets were coming from the workshop. Albert Speer, Minister of Munitions, witnessed the first launch on 13th June but it proved a disaster, as did a second two months later. However, the third rocket flew a successful 190km on 3rd October. Later that year mass production was authorised.

Meanwhile in mid-June 1942 the FZG 76 received approval to progress at highest priority. The Fieseler factory took over the production and models were being tested in December.

In May 1943 both missiles were demonstrated before the military at Peenemünde. The A4 rocket behaved beautifully, but two FZG 76 flights were failures. The Kommission für Fernschiessen (Commission for Long Range Weapons) made exhaustive study of the two missiles and on their recommendation Hitler decided to accelerate development of them both together. They were to be called Revenge Weapons - *Vergeltungswaffen*. The FZG 76 would become the V-1 and the A4 rocket, the V-2.

On the 27th June 1943 the FZG 76 achieved a flight of 234km. The next day Hitler ordered the construction of four massive launching bunkers in northern France.

Hitler's secret weapons had been regarded almost a music hall joke in Britain. But intelligence from spies and photo-reconnaissance were alerting the authorities to something being developed.

Duncan Edwin Duncan-Sandys (1908-1987) was Streatham's Member of Parliament from 1950-1974. In his early years he shot to prominence in the ranks of the Tory Party and even married Winston Churchill's daughter, Diana. From 1935 he was the Member of the Norwood Division of Lambeth. He had been the Commander of Britain's first experimental anti-aircraft rocket unit but was invalided out of the Forces after a motor accident. He returned to the Commons where he was made Minister responsible for weapons research and development. It was with this background that Churchill appointed Sandys to investigate the possible German threat. The "Bodyline" Committee was established, named after the notorious 1933 Cricket Test Series with Australia. It was later to be renamed "Crossbow".

Verification of rocket activity was confirmed with photographs taken on 12th June 1943 by a "Mosquito" aircraft of 540 Squadron. Rockets could be seen on trailers at Peenemünde. Fifteen days later Sandys had sufficient evidence to report to the War Cabinet.

On the night of 17th/18th August 600 planes of Bomber Command, under Operation "Hydra", bombed the installations at Peenemünde. Much damage was done but most of the casualties were amongst the foreign labourers conscripted to work at the site. Peenemünde West, where the V-1 test-flying programme was undertaken, was unscathed. Although much of the plant was salvageable, the Germans decided to move operations to Nordhausen in the Hartz Mountains, which was better protected. The work thus continued but it had been set back.

In November Sandys' responsibilities were transferred to the Deputy Chief of Air Staff, Air Marshall N.H. Bottomley, but he remained as advisor on rockets. In December 1943 the Crossbow Committee was formed to co-ordinate counter measures to the threat still undetermined.

Air reconnaissance revealed a number of strange constructions in northern France. Nicknamed 'ski sites' they were long and straight except for a curve at one end. Ominously, they all pointed towards London. High officials in the A.R.P. and the Royal Observer Corps were quietly informed to keep an eye open for strange flying objects, but for the rest of the population there was a blissful ignorance.

As well as delivering the horrific blanket bombing raids on the German cities of Hamburg, Dresden and Berlin, Allied bombers were beginning to soften up France ready for invasion, but the strange sites received more attention than most. The Germans hastened to camouflage them, and new types of launchers were constructed. The impatient Hitler ordered that England should be assaulted with a combined use of V-1s, bombers and long-range guns. The bombardment would open like a 'thunderclap'. 20th April 1944 was suggested (the Führer's birthday), but the bombing and technical problems frustrated the delivery of the V-1s.

Meanwhile the initiative was with the Allies. The build-up of troops and ships along the south coast was suddenly unleashed across the Channel. Just before dawn on 6th June 1944, troops from Britain, U.S.A., Canada and France secured a foothold on the beaches of Normandy. The Second Front - so eagerly awaited - had been created: Germany began its retreat from the west.

There was much jubilation in Britain, optimistic that the end of the war was in sight. But a word of caution was sent on 7th June by Senior District Warden Kenneth Bryant to all wardens in the Streatham Division:

"The long-awaited Invasion of Western Europe is on, and a grand initial success achieved - but the Prime Minister solemnly warns us against premature optimism.

"We in London, have recently enjoyed a long sequence of Alert-free nights, may it continue, but let us heed and apply Mr Churchill's warning to our own job of Civil Defence. For myself I cannot believe (much as I would like to) that we shall have no further air raids on Streatham.

"Let us, therefore, maintain our preparations in good shape. Let every form of training go forward with increased rather than diminished zeal, so that whatever may lie ahead, we shall discharge our responsibilities to the utmost of our capacity."

Bryant's warning was well timed. Overwhelmed by the Allied might, the Germans pulled back, grudgingly yielding their French territory. Although not fully ready they were forced to play their final hands. A week after D-Day the first revenge weapons were launched.

Four hours later than intended, on the morning of Tuesday 13th June, some ten flying bombs were catapulted towards London. Half of these crashed immediately, another fell in the sea, but the remaining four continued northwards. In England, two R.O.C. observers at a Martello Tower at Dymchurch were quick to realise this strange-sounding aircraft with a glowing tail as the predicted secret weapon. The 'Diver' code-word alerted the defence systems.

At 4.13 a.m. the first V-1 crashed in a field near Swanscombe. Two others fell harmlessly, but the third of the quartet hit a railway bridge in Bethnal Green. Thirty people were injured and six killed. The slaughter had begun.

There was a pause until midday 15th June when some 200 bombs were launched over a 24 hour period. Sixty of these got through to London.

The V-1 Onslaught on Streatham

Streatham received its first V-1 on 16th June when the former Empire Cinema in the High Road took a direct hit. There were no fatalities but the extent of destruction aroused grave foreboding. Even the authorities were unsure what they were dealing with. In the early days of the offensive ministers and military personnel attended each site hoping to salvage clues of the weapon. Streatham was visited by Admiral Sir Edward Evans, one of London's Regional Commissioners. Councillor Willison, Chairman of Wandsworth War Damage Committee, asked Sir Edward what had caused the devastation. He was told: "You don't know and you are not supposed to know."

However, as more weapons crashed or flew overhead the nature of the beast became common knowledge to military and civilians alike.

Flying almost in a straight line, the V-1 made a relatively easy target. Anti-aircraft guns were able to account for many, especially when proximity fuses were added to the shells. Many of the faster fighter planes - and jet-propelled "Meteors" were coming into service - were able to attack the flying bombs without reprisal - provided the pilot disengaged before the warhead exploded! The problem of ack-ack and fighters operating in the same airspace was soon apparent. In mid-July, in a matter of a few days, nearly 1000 pieces of artillery were transported from all over the country to the Channel coast, leaving the skies overland free for purely aircraft attacks. Fighters also patrolled over the open seas. Balloons increased threefold during July, and some hundreds of V-1s were brought down as the wings snagged the cables. It was a formidable gauntlet and was ultimately to account for some 40% of the "doodlebugs", which the RAF were to nickname them.

Despite the Allied bombing of the launching sites, railway supply lines and factories, the launching crews were able to keep up a more-or-less continuous barrage. A good crew could send a V-1 racing up the ramp every 30 minutes, and sites averaged some 15 missiles daily, regardless of the weather, day and night. Tower Bridge was the aiming point but any 'near miss' within 5 miles was certain to find a target. The route to London over Sussex and Kent was to become known as 'doodlebug alley', and the landscape was pock-marked by missiles brought down by the defences.

Almost as many crashed through malfunction. But behind the statistics lie the enormity of the terror, since of the 9251 bombs that crossed the coast, some 60% fell on land and nearly half of these in the densely built-up London region.

On crashing to earth at the end of its 25 minute flight, the warhead exploded with terrific devastation. In a densely built-up area some dozen houses would be totally obliterated, and the blast could affect as many as a thousand neighbouring homes to a greater or lesser degree. Much of the peripheral damage was confined to roofs and windows. Slates were stripped off and glass disintegrated. Indeed, most injuries were caused by flying glass. The blast played many strange tricks, sparing nearby objects but smashing others more distant.

In the early days of the onslaught, the siren was sounded at each approach. As they became more numerous, the value of this warning was self-defeating. In larger factories and offices too much time was lost waiting an 'all clear' that watchers were employed to monitor the buzz bomb and give warning only if there was a likelihood of its approaching the area.

However, it did not take long for people to appreciate the inherent warning given by the machine itself. The characteristic drone was sufficient to

Headlines of the *Streatham News* following the first attacks

THE DOODLEBUG SUMMER IN STREATHAM

	JUNE	JULY	AUGUST
Monday	5 12 19 [26]	[3][10] 17 24 31	7 14 21 28
Tuesday	6 13 20 27	4 11 [18] 25	[1] 8 15 22 29
Wednesday	7 14 21 [28]	[5] 12 19 26	2 [9] 16 23 30
Thursday	1 8 15 [22][29]	[6][13] 20 [27]	[3] 10 17 24 31
Friday	2 9 [16][23][30]	7 14 [21] 28	4 11 18 25
Saturday	3 10 17 [24]	[1][8] 15 [22] 29	[5] 12 19 26
Sunday	4 11 [18] 25	2 9 16 [23] 30	[6][13] 20 27

□ Single Bomb   ▢ 2-4 Bombs

announce its presence. But as the craft nosed downwards to its destruction, the engine cut out. During the few seconds of silence was the time to scramble under any available cover. Apart from developing an acute sense of hearing, Londoners became conscious of a less honourable trait: the guilt of wishing destruction of their neighbours, as they silently prayed for the Angel of Death to pass them by.

As during the Blitz, the positive "Britain can take it!" image was promoted and certainly there was much heroism and bravery, especially amongst the rescue squads. But the drain on civilian morale was great. The fear instilled is brought vividly to life in the letter transcribed opposite.

There was, of course, complete censorship about the raids. Newspaper reports spoke merely of events "somewhere in southern England". It was not desirable for the launching crews to know their weapons were reaching the targets. The Luftwaffe was denied air space for aerial reconnaissance, so controlled spies were fed elaborate disinformation to give the impression the V-1s were overshooting central London. Impact times of southern falls were re-allocated to northern boroughs. Newspaper "Deaths" columns - which previously indicated a scatter of "enemy action" fatalities centred on Streatham Hill - were rationed to only three entries to any one postal district. The objective was to persuade the Germans to reduce their range mechanisms by some 4%, with the consequence that Croydon and surrounding districts suffered as the bombs fell short of their intended target.

Any persons not engaged in necessary work were encouraged to leave the metropolis. An evacuation programme was hurriedly re-introduced similar to that at the beginning of the war. The Ministry of Health arranged for billets for school children, mothers with a child under 5 years of age, and expectant mothers. This was extended in early August to mothers with children at school age. A free travel voucher and billeting allowance was provided for those categories, and also for the elderly, infirm and blind people who made their own arrangements to live with relatives and friends.

Crowds of schoolchildren - some with their mothers - waiting for trains to evacuate them were a familiar sight at London rail stations throughout July. Although sad at leaving, there must have been relief at fleeing from the danger to live in beautiful countryside.

The Streatham News reported the welcome given by the Mayor of Lancaster to hundreds of "Vacees" as they arrived from London one Sunday afternoon in July. The children passed to the rest centres where they were able to wash and freshen-up and then enjoy a hot meal provided by the emergency feeding centre. Fifty percent of the children were allocated billets in that city and the remainder sent to the surrounding rural areas.

Evacuation was sometimes a trial both to the unaccompanied children and their temporary foster parents. The Chief Billeting Officer from Newton-le-Willows admitted that some people who expressed their willingness to receive evacuees into their homes were totally unable to look after their own families. There was also an incredulity on the part of the hosts who, because of the playing down of the issue in the media, could not appreciate the scale of the damage. An instance was reported in *The Streatham News* of homeless south Londoners turning up at the door of the Midlands family they had sheltered during the Blitz, only to be accused of exaggeration: "You South Englanders are yellow!"

The larger schools made arrangements for their pupils to amalgamate temporarily with provincial academic establishments. Battersea Grammar School (of Abbotswood Road) went to Hertford Grammar School. The Streatham Hill & Clapham High School had sent a party to Halifax, and in mid-August was preparing to send more. However, some preferred to brave the situation rather than suffer the trauma of evacuation. Some pupils of the Streatham Grammar School sat - and passed - the Cambridge School Certificate examination held in July as the V-1s flew overhead. Others deferred the exams to take them in December.

For some of the children who remained, there was tragedy. *The Streatham News* reported the pathetic sight of a six-year old girl playing with a ball and the leg of a table amid the ruins of her home, innocently unaware her parents had recently been killed.

As the consequences of the new terror became quickly apparent, residents returned to the Blitz habit of sleeping in the public shelters, although during the day everyone carried on work as usual. Here, perhaps, is the point to pay brief tribute to the shelter wardens of Streatham. Perhaps not so hazardous a job as most

Living with the Bombs

19 Trinity Rise
SW2
July 4th 1944

Dear Evelyn,

I dare say that anyone in the country who has any friends - (however vague the friendship!) in London, must be wondering how we are getting on.

Well it is frankly grim - the only thing is that is so inevitable and unavoidable that one just endures - one can't do anything else! I won't enlarge much but I feel sure that some little detail will help you to understand what this part of the front line is like.

Here is a typical day's experience.

Aroused from a short sleep about 7 by the usual wail of siren - then in the distance the faint hum, which gradually grows louder till it gets to the pitch of a gigantic hornet out to sting. It may pass us by at a distance. or it may come "right over" and that terms includes about ½ miles radius on each side. One listens for the engine to stop. If it stops before it reaches the overhead area there is the breathless wait for the explosion. Sometimes it follows in a second or two if the Flying bomb drops quickly - but sometimes the F.B. glides quite a distance (probably towards one!) before exploding. If it reaches overhead there is still the breathless hope that it will carry on a few seconds of flying to take it out of blast range. This keying up and relaxing takes places at every bomb which comes within a mile either side. We may have 7 or 8 before breakfast and another lot during the rest of the morning - a whole bunch about midday when people are in the streets - a few in the afternoon and another big lot in the early evening. We generally get a lull in the early part of the night, then from 12 o'clock till 3 or 4, then a break till about 6 or 7 o'clock.

It means we get very little sleep, and get our work interfered with, as we must take cover - to some extent - while the bomb is coming and till we hear the explosion.

It isn't comfortable travelling - tho' of course we have to go about our duties - just hoping we shan't be caught.

Several times when travelling in London or homewards I have heard the bomb stop and the crash has sounded behind where I have just come from.

We have no shelter here at all. There is no basement that would be safe, but I have made some kind of shutter protection against flying glass in the bedrooms and at the end of the lobby so that we can rest in moderate security from risk of distant blast. Nothing could save us from direct hit or near blast. In the day, Miss Ashford stands in the lobby - and when I am home I crouch by the dining room door - or under the big table with a large sofa cushion to put over my face - or to fall flat on to. In the office, our small kitchen has had the window wired and as it is an entirely inside room, it is reasonably safe. It is the best we can do. We could not possibly spend the best part of the day in the basement shelter which was made for the old type of air raid which was of short and certain duration.

In the 20 days we have been having these raids there have been at least 30 bombs within about a mile of this house. Streatham-Streatham Hill have had it even worse and we get the sound of that - even if we don't get the rock of the house.

As an illustration of the damage that is done. Where a bomb actually hits a house, 2 or 3 others each side are also wrecked, houses opposite - or if short gardens - at the back, also are practically wrecked. 10 to 12 on either side of that and opposite will lose all windows - frames and doors and most of the plaster - and for about ¼ mile all round most of the window glass goes.

A large number have fallen in central London and on all the suburbs - but of course - South and South East and East are the worst.

Some of the working class people spend most of their time in the shelters or underground railways. They are turned out of the latter on the all clear and simply sit on the pavements or seats near till the next alert. During the day we have a fresh alert every time another group of F.B.s get through the defences. As soon as they have all been accounted for we get an all clear. We may get 3 or 4 in a morning or an afternoon, but on the heavy cloudy days sometimes we have an alert for several hours, and usually continuously the best part of the night. How we long for clear skies and moonlight nights!

It sounds grim and is so, but it has its lighter side. For instance it is quite difficult to have a bath! We manage it during a lull, with one of us posted at an upper south window from where we can hear the distant warning which comes about 1-2 minutes before ours which is generally about 1 minute before the bomb comes within sound. The 2 or 3 minutes warning is enough for the bather to whisk out of the bath and into some reasonable garb. Once the explosion is heard one may risk getting back on the chance that it one stray one - but it is a risk that is not likely taken!

On Saturday which was a bad afternoon for us, I was doing some [sewing] machining and in the space of about ¾ hour I had to retire under the dining room table 6 times for near visitors! Each time the house simply rocked - but still our windows are intact!

Don't laugh or say she's making it up, but just as I wrote that sentence, I had to dive under the table with my face in a cushion!

Well, that is a long chat, just to explain the real reason for my writing. We are worried about Anne - Bert's girl - who is at Boarding School at Gadolphin, Salisbury. She is just 15 and we don't like the idea of her coming home for 2 months to the conditions I have described. There would be little for her to do and it would be very nerve wracking. Do you know anywhere she could be fixed up?

On the whole I keep going. Full time job, household chores and lots of gardening with Girl Guide work when Hitler permits.

My love to you

Marion

A letter from Marion Cable written during the period of the Flying Bombs from just over the Streatham border of Civil Defence, it was certainly an exacting one. For the first time ever, Streatham shelters were full to capacity as extensive damage to housing and the unpredictability of the V-1s brought residents to seek security. Every night there were problems to be settled, differences between shelterers, missing and damaged equipment, registers to be checked and a dozen minor duties. It was difficult to satisfy everybody. Through the constant nervous tension, people were generally rather 'edgy' and shelter wardens, with patience, tact and good humour, did a lot to maintain the high standard of morale with which the public using the shelters faced their ordeal. Mr Dineen in "I" District, Major Firth in "J" and Mr Hack in "K", all worked hard and did well; whilst special mention must be made of the Deputy Divisional Shelter Officer (Miss J.C.McEwen) who provided efficient liaison with Headquarters, Wandsworth.

The comradeship evident during the Blitz displayed itself again in this crisis. Those not affected turned out to help their less fortunate neighbours with the aid of hammers, saws, brooms, cups of tea and offers of asylum for household treasures.

Those people staying put tried to live as normally as possible, travelling to work daily. Tram crews were admired for their coolness. An instance is reported that as a flying bomb approached, a tram conductor turned to his passengers and rapped out "lie down - away from the windows", while he stood on the platform ready to give the "Raiders passed."

The normal delivery of newspapers, milk and letters each day was a striking feature of the period - shopkeepers, too, remained open for "Business as usual", even if customers were fewer. The Locarno dance hall and cinemas were always available to patrons, of whom there were no small number. The Streatham Hill Theatre continued with twice-daily variety until a bomb put them out of action.

Despite reduced numbers, many institutions carried on. The Darby & Joan Club, formed only a couple of years earlier, continued to be run by a dedicated team of ladies determined the members should have a haven during the day, away from their lonely homes or the public shelters. Some 40 older people arrived each morning for a bath or wash-up. A mid-day meal and high tea were provided. They spent what time they could - between alerts - in the garden, some even playing on the putting green. Indeed, one member, Mrs Beatrice Dunbar who had joined in March, developed sufficient skill to win the year's ladies' singles championship which was held during the V-1 summer. Later in the year she became engaged to her instructor, Albert Davies. Four men acted as spotters on a rota. When danger approached, the spotter on duty would ring a hand bell in the garden and a dinner gong in the house. The members then trooped into the coal cellars which were converted into shelters. Often the meals were served below, as were religious services.

Fortunately, apart from a few broken windows and coping, the building suffered no damage.

Other organisations were affected when their venues were hit. Several churches were put out of action from blast damage, although a crypt could often serve as a place of worship. Some groups felt it wiser to suspend their operations for the period. Whether it was because of the evacuation of so many residents, loss of households, or lack of manpower, is not specified for the almost 50% drop in War Savings during the bomb months. However, the Births' columns of *The Streatham News* during March to June 1945 did not reveal any local slackening of certain activity.

Whilst most people displayed courage, there also existed greed. Times of hardship always encourages theft, and damaged property provided easy targets. Gangs of youths would descend on incident sites picking up valuables whilst others' attentions were distracted by humanitarian needs. Most distasteful were reports from owners lying trapped beneath the rubble hearing looters working through their homes: clothes were removed from wardrobes, eggs from under hens.

Much of the petty thieving could have been done by children for whom wrecked houses provided an adventure playground, full of fascinating objects. Whilst some thefts might have been opportunist, others were more calculating, stooping to elaborate deceptions, even in broad daylight. An instance was reported of men with a cart claiming to have been sent by the local council to remove furniture - since facilities for storing salvaged items existed. The woman of the house, still under the shock of the blast gratefully accepted the offer, never to see them again. The blight was not uniform. In a ruined house in Valley Road, antique furniture was left untouched; but in Streatham Vale, even fences were being stolen. The theft of a mirror worth £2 procured a month's gaol sentence for the offender, and other cases reported in the Press showed the severity with which the crime was dealt.

The problem meant that some victims felt it necessary to stay in the area rather than evacuate to safety. With wardens and police already fully occupied, the Home Guard were asked to patrol bombed sites at night to prevent looting. Residents also formed vigilante patrols.

Many of us would gladly die for our Families
But can we Live with them ?
Victory Homes need more than bricks and mortar.
Victory Homes are production centres for the
How ? Come to   SPIRIT THAT WINS.
THE VICTORY HOMES CAMPAIGN
Sundays, 6.30 p.m. JULY 15—24th Week Nights, 8 p.m.
IN THE LARGE MARQUEE
IMMANUEL CHURCH GARDEN
(Facing Streatham Common on the High Road).
Challenging Speakers.   Questions Invited.

The War Ends

The last V-1 to fall on Streatham was on 13th August at Furzedown. As the Allies overran the French sites, the campaign gradually finished. Elsewhere, there were a few incidents of V-1s launched over the North Sea from Heinkel bombers.

However, London was soon to be targeted by the V-2 rockets. Having a longer range, being easier to camouflage and easier to transport, and not requiring permanent launching pads, these rockets were to prove a greater menace. Whilst the warhead was only marginally larger than that of the V-1, the real terror of this weapon was the inability to defend against it. All conventional anti-aircraft defence was useless. With the missile travelling faster than the speed of sound, there was no warning: it announced itself by the sudden explosion on impact, followed seconds later by the noise of its descent which eerily vanished.

The V-2 campaign commenced on 8th September. Altogether there were 1115 incidents in England, nearly half of which fell on London. Streatham was fortunately spared this onslaught. The nearest V-2 fell on Tooting Bec Common on 5th November.

By 28th March 1945 all German bombardment of England ceased. Squeezed between the Russians in the east and the Allies in the west, Nazi resistance doggedly persisted through the streets of Berlin until the surrender. On 8th May Britain erupted in a wave of ecstasy. As the crowds in Streatham celebrated VE-day, one particular bonfire was singled out for Press comment: that on the site of the old Empire Cinema, the first victim of the V-1s. People stayed up late that night, perhaps watching the flames with a mixture of relief and sad memories of the destruction. In the early hours a derelict car was hauled onto the fire.

Victory against the Germans had long been regarded as inevitable and the state of emergency ceased. The "Forgotten War" raged still in the Far East, but for the British civilians it was over. Life slowly groped towards a normality.

The Vicar of Immanuel Church recognised that peace would create a vast social problem as families, torn apart by war reunited as strangers to each other, changed by their experiences and by trying conditions not amenable to reconciliation. Rev. O.K. de Berry launched a Victory Homes Campaign, a week of events starting on 15th July 1945 with a special service at the church. This was followed by the first of many evening meetings in a large marquee erected in the church garden. Every night ordinary men and women were to discuss their problems and this was followed by an eminent speaker on such themes as "Victory starts in the home" and "Foundations of the home".

The Home Guard had stood down on 31st December 1944, their function having been fulfilled. When the V-2 offensive finished, other A.R.P. units were wound down. The Heavy Rescue retained a few men at Coventry Hall, but most others involved themselves in war damage work. On 24th April the Central Firewatching Party held a sale of surplus equipment at the Dolcis Shoe Company, selling amongst other items, tin helmets at 1/- (5p) a dozen for use as flower pots!

Things would never be the same, but the fear of bombing was gone. Indeed, the memories of the terror of war was being salved and the events could be seen with a detached fascination and a relief of having survived them.

First among the local memoirs came Kenneth Bryant's *Streatham's 41*. Drawing directly from his own experience, the booklet provided a unique history of the events of the Doodlebug Summer. The book was published on 16th March 1945 and the run of 5000 sold out in 30 hours. A 'black market' rose with copies passing at five times the cover price of 1/-. The text was illustrated with photographs donated by Denis Thiel of the South Thames Press Agency and Peter Eastman, the staff photographer of *The Streatham News*. The cover artwork was done by Stewart Skingle, and his firm at St.John's Hill, Clapham, did the printing, the cost being funded by South London Motors. Any profits from the sales were given to the Prisoners-of-War section of the Streatham Comforts Fund, a charity set up at the beginning of the war to cater for the needs of local servicemen, both at the battlefront and behind wire. The number of copies had been restricted by shortage of paper, but a further reprint was made on 7th May.

The V-1 was a feature at the Trade Exhibition held in the late autumn of 1945. 9000 people attended the exhibition of how the local industries planned to meet the needs of a peaceful economy and also their many war effort schemes not generally known. The South London Motors workshop, where the exhibition was held, produced a half-scale model of a V-1 complete with flaming tail which stood in the forecourt. Inside the building films were shown including one of the V-1 attacks and the defences. There was also a display of photographs showing bomb damage in Streatham and full details of the 'alarm within the alert' scheme which saved thousands of hours of production time.

The Civil Defence had stood up to the enemy's might, but it was no longer required. On 10th May the men assembled at Sunnyhill Road School to be inspected by the Royal Family in their Victory peregrinations round the suburbs. A month later - on 10th June - they were officially disbanded. Then came the process of clearing up, terminating with the closing at the end of July of Divisional Office at Streatham Baths with Miss J.C.McEwen ("Miss Mack") handing over the keys to Mr Smith,the Baths Superintendent.

Kenneth Bryant was later awarded the B.E.M. for his services to the A.R.P. and the people of Streatham.

Wandsworth Borough Council—Streatham Division.

POST RAID ASSISTANCE

Temporary Arrangements

1. REPAIRS TO HOUSES, ETC.

The Borough Housing Department are doing their utmost to catch up with the First Aid Repair position. Men and material are automatically sent to all bombed roads as fresh incidents occur and IT IS NOT NECESSARY FOR OCCUPIERS TO TAKE ANY STEPS THEMSELVES to notify the need for these First Aid Repairs, the parties will come round as quickly as possible (in some cases materials are available free for those who can do their own repairs).

Within 30 days of the damage occurring a C.1 Form should be sent to the War Damage Commission. Supplies of these forms are usually available at 7 HOPTON PARADE (the Fire Guard Office, opposite Streatham Baths). Hours 9 a.m. to 8 p.m. daily. All other enquiries about House Repairs should be made there. Phone: STR. 0990

2. ASSISTANCE BOARD.

ST. LEONARD'S CHURCH HALL,—Monday to Saturday, Hours 9-0 a.m. to 5-0 p.m. Cash advances against War Damage Claims (excluding House property). Also War Injury claims, and relief of acute financial distress from War causes. Issue of replacement Clothing Coupons and permits to purchase curtains.

3. RE-HOUSING.

SHOP, 1 BRIDGE PARADE (opposite Streatham Station)—Hours 9-0 a.m. to 7-0 p.m. daily ;

or EARDLEY ROAD REST CENTRE, BLEGBOROUGH ROAD (off Mitcham Lane).—Hours 9-0 a.m. to 8-0 p.m. daily.

Whilst efforts are being made to requisition further properties, the problem is very difficult, for Streatham was practically "full-up" before these raids commenced. It will assist if applicants can notify the address of any empty property that would suit them.

4 BILLETING.

BILLETING OFFICER. EARDLEY ROAD REST CENTRE, BLEGBOROUGH ROAD (off Mitcham Road).—Hours 9-0 a.m. to 8-0 p.m. daily.

(a) Billeting Addresses in Streatham are available for bombed-out persons.

(b) Those who have made their own arrangements to stay with friends can see about the billeting allowances here or BRIDGE PARADE (opposite Streatham Station).

5. EVACUATION.

(a) All classes of persons who have been "bombed-out" (i.e. home no longer habitable) and have an address at which they know they can be accommodated, can secure free travel vouchers and permits to enter (most) banned areas, also certificates of Homelessness, which will facilitate payment of billeting allowance from :—

Mr. COLLINS, BRIDGE PARADE (opposite Streatham Station).—Hours 9-0 a.m. to 6-0 p.m. daily.

(b) Mothers, with children of school age or under, who have been rendered homeless by bombing, or similar homeless expectant mothers, can now register for evacuation at any Rest Centre—where the necessary certificate of Homelessness can also be obtained on production of National Registration Identity Cards.

(NOTE.—Billets will be found and transport arranged for registered applicants under this L.C.C. scheme)

Nearest Centre :—EARDLEY RD. SCHOOL, BLEGBOROUGH RD. (off Mitcham Lane). Hours : 9 a.m. to 8 p.m. daily.

6. SHELTERS.

Morrison Table Shelters.—Application Forms at Streatham Baths. Shelters delivered as available.

Public Shelters.—The various Shelter Wardens who are in charge of each Shelter at night, will advise on current bunk position and reservations.

7. FURNITURE REMOVAL AND STORAGE.

Removals free from severely damaged houses, or Contractors' accounts reimbursed up to £10, also free storage arranged if required.

6 HOPTON PARADE, S.W.16 (opposite Streatham Baths). Tel. STR. 1929. Hours : 10-0 a.m. to 6-0 p.m. daily

8. REST CENTRE.

Apply any Wardens' Post or W.V.S. for nearest available accommodation, as this will vary from time to time.

9. EMERGENCY TRANSPORT FOR "BOMBED-OUT" PERSONS.

In suitable cases (e.g. invalids and aged persons) where other transport is unobtainable, the W.V.S. can usually arrange for a V.C.P. car to make the trip, if not too far.

Apply W.V.S., 128 HIGH ROAD (near G.P.O.) Hours : 10-0 a.m. to 5-0 p.m. (Monday to Saturday).

Or any W.V.S. Enquiry Point when operating at Incidents.

10. W.V.S. CLOTHING DEPOT.

151 STREATHAM HIGH ROAD (opposite St. Leonard's Church). Hours : 9-30 a.m. to 4-30 p.m. (Mon. to Sat.).

11. ENQUIRIES re CASUALTIES.

1. Nearest Police Station.
2. W.V.S. Enquiry Point on Incident (whilst operating).
3. Warden's Post nearest Incident.
4. Streatham Baths.

(NOTE.—Information can only be given to relatives, etc.).

12. CITIZENS' ADVICE BUREAU.

ST. LEONARD'S CHURCH HALL—Monday, Wednesday and Friday, 9-30 a.m. to 12-30 p.m.

13. FOOD OFFICE for Emergency Ration Books, etc.

TUDOR HALL, PINFOLD ROAD, STREATHAM, S.W.16. Hours : 9-0 a.m. to 5-30 p.m.

14. MISCELLANEOUS ENQUIRIES also Baby Gas Helmets issued.

STREATHAM BATHS. Hours : 9-0 a.m. to 9-0 p.m. daily (other Gas Masks at any Wardens' Post).

15. BOROUGH INFORMATION CENTRE.

THE TOWN HALL, (foot of) EAST HILL, WANDSWORTH, S.W.18.

DIVISIONAL OFFICE, STREATHAM BATHS.   7th July, 1944

(K.B.)

Counting the Cost

Of the 5208 flying bombs that evaded the anti-aircraft defences, 2419 reached the Greater London area. They caused a casualty rate higher than that of the 1940/41 Blitz. However, this was because many more were injured - especially by flying glass - and the total of deaths at 5122 was actually lower. The worst hit London borough was Croydon with 142 missiles. This was followed by Wandsworth with 122, then Lewisham with 114. Lambeth had 72 and Camberwell, 81.

London's worst single incident during this period was the bombing of the crowded Chapel of Wellington Barracks, Birdcage Walk, Westminster, when 121 people were killed on June 18th. On the same date, Wandsworth received its worst incident at Quill Edge when 34 died.

Streatham, with its share of 41 bombs, had casualties listed as 986, of which 335 were seriously injured and 567 slightly injured. Some injured were to die later, and no doubt many others' lives were shortened. The 84 deaths (as given at the time) averaged 2 per bomb (just below the London average). But most of the bombs did not claim deaths; only 22 doing so, the highest single instance being 12 fatalities (Bomb 35 at Pendle Road).

Sir Ernest Gowers, Senior Regional Commissioner, visited the site of Streatham's last bomb, having just come from another borough in which there had been an incident with very heavy casualties. Discussing this with the Senior District Warden, the latter said, "Well, in that respect we've been lucky." Sir Ernest replied, "I certainly never expected to hear anyone in Wandsworth say they have been lucky with fly bombs!" But in truth, when considering the occasions in other areas when bombs hit crowded places, then from a casualty standpoint, things in Streatham might have been much worse.

Whilst many residents evacuated to friends, others stayed in the area, living in the ruins of their homes or in the public shelters. The first priority by the authorities had always been to make houses rehabitable as quickly as feasible. After each incident immediate steps were taken to salvage furniture and household goods, putting them in store for future use. To prevent further damage from the elements, roofs were covered, windows boarded up and services restored to those residents sitting tight. The Home Guard and the N.F.S. quickly organised flying squads to repair homes. During the first ten days of the onslaught, nearly 5000 tiles were replaced by local men, perhaps a Sisyphean task as the bombing continued.

Within seven hours of the first V-1, Wandsworth Council applied to the Ministry of Labour for 1000 extra labourers to be allocated for the area to deal with the damage. As the days passed, this request quickly rose to 5000! From across the country builders, carpenters, plumbers and electricians were drafted into London. Work gangs were quartered in hut encampments. The more fortunate were occasionally received into people's homes, but on the whole there was a reluctance by residents to accommodate these men. Complaints were common that the men were too old, or too young and inexperienced, and other were not physically fit. Of course, the really able-bodied men were in the Forces.

Some 600 naval ratings, awaiting drafting, were also brought in by the Ministry of Works to alleviate the labour shortage. Their presence and their workmanship were occasionally criticised, but most appreciated the services of these "Doodlebug Matelots". A letter in *The Streatham News* from a Mrs Price-Lloyd welcomed "the boys' cheery humour like a breath of sea air. By working in the pouring rain and ignoring the sirens they saved hundreds of pounds-worth of damage as the house was open to the sky. I made quarts of tea and lots of bread and damson jam. I even accompanied them on the piano with *By Aggie's Ship's Side*."

Despite the Council allocating Streatham half of their available workforce, the repairs seemed as shambolic as the ruins on which they worked. The major problem was the acute shortage of materials. Nails and tarpaulins were scarce, and only a ninth of the required plasterboard could be found. Clear glass was in short supply and black felt was nailed in remaining windows once the quota was used. Many of the labourers were idle because of these deficiencies and, residents claimed, lack of supervision. Jobs were left uncompleted as men were shunted from district to district. But there was little shortage of paperwork as bureaucracy burgeoned: incidents were cited of time wasted because of the wrong colour form.

The range of problems the new conditions caused necessitated they be tackled accordingly. It is perhaps a measure of success at meeting the challenge that so many help lines were available. A leaflet was hastily prepared by the Civil Defence Divisional Office to guide the bewildered victim through the bureaucracy (reproduced opposite). It was so useful that two revised versions were issued.

The War Damage Commission was responsible for compensation on damage to land and buildings. To claim for repairs in excess of £5, Form C1 had to be returned within 30 days of the incident. To ease the problem of Streathamites having to trudge to Wandsworth Town Hall to deal with the claims, a more local Assistance Board was set up at St.Leonard's Hall thanks to the Rev. D.M.Salmon. A uniformed mobile team of the Board was summoned from Birmingham and they opened operations 9.30 a.m. on Tuesday 20th June. The Salvation Army was on hand to supply cups of tea, and the paper work was amicably and quickly dealt with.

A Government-imposed £10 limit on private work introduced in October prevented the more skilled labourers employed by local smaller builders from making any effective contribution. The Council was also slow in paying bills for work done.

The Streatham Ratepayers' Association called a meeting on 11th November 1944 at Dunraven School. Frustration by residents made this the most lively and vociferous meeting ever held. Councillor W.D.Willison, Chairman of the Wandsworth War Damage Committee, spoke of the situation, stating that in the borough as a whole, 59,398 houses were damaged, of which Streatham had 24,143 (40%), yet 3835 men (some 49% of total available) were engaged in repairs. Unresponsive to the explanations, the members of the meeting passed two motions: expressing dissatisfaction with the progress on repairs and calling for the release of skilled men from the armed forces; and demanding the reinstatement of properties to their former conditions by the War Damage Commission.

Not everyone had cause for complaint. Today, Irene Booth of Cricklade Avenue, is still grateful for the care taken to restore her ornate ceiling when expedience would have favoured cheaper short cuts. Despite the criticisms, the Council claimed to reach the Ministry of Health's winter target of 47,000 repaired homes in the borough by March 1945.

Apart from homes, there was also a priority to rebuild hospitals, nursing homes and doctors' surgeries. Business premises were less favoured, and the Streatham & District Chamber of Commerce met on 23rd October at the White Lion to discuss the plight of its members, many of whom had been unable to trade since their shops were hit. George Mason, the tobacconist at 124 Streatham Hill, felt particularly victimised in being affected by blast fives times within two weeks during June. The Ministry later decided that shops dealing with foodstuffs could receive some encouragement. At the other extreme, places of entertainment, like the Streatham Hill Theatre and the Gaumont Palace Cinema, were continually denied permission for rebuilding until many years after the war. They had to wait until 1950 and 1955 respectively before reopening.

War damage insurance for goods, furniture, clothing and other personal belongings were dealt with by the Board of Trade through the respective insurance companies. However, a victim of three attacks living in Barcombe Avenue was informed that no claims could be settled until the end of the war but he could apply to the Public Assistance Broad for an advance.

In cases of hardship, the local Assistance Board could offer immediate financial aid and the replacement of essential items like furniture, clothing, spectacles and dentures, and tradesmen's tools. The Lord Mayor's Air Raid Distress Fund was especially active during the V-1 period. The State would bury victims without charge to the relatives, or a grant of £10 was available towards a private funeral. A widow could obtain a 10-week temporary allowance of 50/- (£2.50) on the death of her husband, and children disabled by enemy action would be able to claim a pension at the age of 15.

With damaged homes prey to the elements, residents' miseries were exacerbated by a coal shortage during the particularly cold winter which followed. The V-1 attacks were blamed as contributing to the problem. Households were limited to 5 cwt a month. At a dump in the car park of the Regal Cinema (now the ABC), Civil Defence workers - jokingly calling themselves "Bevan Boys" - helped to shovel coal into sacks for customers.

The Women's Voluntary Service did much to provide for the victims of the bombing. Bundles for Britain had been sent from the U.S.A. and kept in depots. When the emergency arose this clothing was distributed to those who were unable to salvage any from their homes. Late in the war, W.V.S. branches throughout the country rallied to the Londoners' plight. Gloucester area Region 7 adopted Battersea, Lambeth and Wandsworth as part of the Re-homing Scheme for London. All kinds of household equipment were trundled in from the West Country - from Bristol to Buddleigh Salterton. By mid-March 1945 some 70 van loads of gifts weighing 350 tons, from pianos to clothes pegs, were unloaded at East Hill central depot. These were allocated to bomb victims by a points system related to the size of the family and degree of hardship. The W.V.S. centre at 18 High Parade, Streatham High Road, was available to householders to register and obtain their green card which enabled them to choose the items they most needed. However, there were so many pictures, these were given away without subtracting points. The Mayor of Wandsworth visited Bristol to thank the people for their generosity.

W.V.S. volunteers sorting out furniture received from the West Country

The Rebuilding of Streatham

If the bombing had left indelible memories on the survivors, then, with an estimated 88% of buildings effected in Streatham, the scars on the landscape also persisted. The process of healing was slow and fraught with problems. The aftermath remains much of the story of the V-1 onslaught as the actual bombing.

Much property damage had been caused by the conventional bombing of the 1940/41 Blitz, and later in the mini-Blitz of early 1944. Confident that the war was soon to be won, the British authorities looked to take the opportunity of sweeping away the ruins and with them some Victorian slums, to rebuild a capital worthy of a triumphant nation. A committee was set up by Sir Patrick Abercrombie, a professor of Town Planning. In 1944 the Greater London Plan was published setting out a broad vision of housing, industry, open spaces and transport.

The additional devastation of the Vengeance weapons compounded the housing problems, and the impending victory would result in the demobilisation of hundreds of thousands of men demanding places to live. After the war, economic growth proved to be slow, possibly because of the expense of the Labour Government's sweeping social reforms, but certainly because of the massive debt repayment to the U.S.A. for their supplies during the war. Utopia was shelved as more expedient measures were adopted.

Where structures were deemed salvageable, they were strengthened and rebuilt, the patching-up imperceptible, except to the knowing eye. Those beyond repair - and those surviving but standing in the way of grander schemes - were razed and new buildings put in their place. For the next decade or so, blocks of flats were erected that transformed the landscape. The Brixton Hill and Upper Tulse Hill area has been wholly rebuilt as a result of the bombing, as also the central regions of Streatham Park. At other sites, 1950's infill mark the spots.

Today, only one bomb-site still remains undeveloped - that opposite the War Memorial (Bomb 23). Only one memorial presently exists to the bombing - that on the rebuilt Streatham Hill & Clapham High School for Girls (Bomb 33) (below).

> AFTER BEING BOMBED ON
> 27 JULY 1944
> THIS BUILDING WAS RE-OPENED
> 22 OCTOBER 1952 BY
> HRH THE DUCHESS OF GLOUCESTER

Faced with the shortage of building materials, the Government proposed temporary houses to be erected on the razed sites. These were mainly of reinforced concrete which came in kits of pre-fabricated elements. The "Pre-fab" was soon to become part of common parlance, but the concept of factory-prepared buildings had existed for over a hundred years previously. Streatham had adopted pre-fabricated iron churches during the mid-Victorian period. Packaged houses were shipped to the emerging colonies to facilitate rapid establishment of settlers. Europe adopted the concept, and Germans especially developed them for rehousing after the Great War of 1914-18. Gropius, and other refugees from the Nazis, improved their status, and the United States manufactured thousands to meet the problems of the 1930's Depression and for housing the increased workforce of armaments factories .

Of the half-dozen models of pre-fabs adopted by the Government for distribution, Wandsworth approved of the Uni-Seco variety. The cost was £250 each, making it one of the cheapest. Its built-in obsolescence was to ensure its early replacement when conditions improved and thereby prevent slums developing. Alarm was caused when the Government decided to manufacture only 3000, allocating a mere 175 to the borough. Wandsworth were forced to buy in also the Portal huts, a style they had formerly opposed. Costing over £650 and with a life expectancy of twenty years, it was feared the huts might be accepted as permanent homes.

Apart from the bomb sites, the fringes of Streatham and Tooting Bec Commons were laid out into estates of 8 and 3 acres, respectively. By early January 1945 the first assignments were being completed. General Eisenhower promised aid of several thousand U.S. engineers to help with the task of demolition and rehabilitation. One group erected the 14 Uni-Seco huts in Gracefield Gardens. They were used to this style of housing from Tennessee, and six men took a mere six hours to erect a hut once the foundations were ready. Apart from frost no weather conditions were allowed to hinder the work. Corporal Groser of the team stated, "We never expected to come over here to do this sort of work. Still, we are very versatile!"

The first Uni-Seco huts to be completed in Streatham were the five in Besley Street. By early February 1945 the new residents were able to confirm they were warm and comfortable. One of the tenants was Mrs Elliott who had lived 30 years in a house on the site before it was destroyed on 3rd July.

A month later - on 15th March - the temporary homes at the junction of Sherwood Avenue and Drakewood Road were officially opened by the Mayor. The W.V.S. arranged for a furniture van from the housing scheme, decorated with red, white and blue ribbons, to distribute small gifts of cushions and ornaments amongst the new residents.

Although the exteriors were not architecturally attractive, they were compact, with a sitting room, two bedrooms, a kitchen and a lavatory - but no bathroom.

The rent for the pre-fabs was 17/6d a week inclusive, requiring a subsidy of £1 from the local authority.

Not all were pleased by the prospect of these novel homes. The L.C.C. hastened the pace by compulsorily purchasing the blitzed sites to erect the huts. Many residents felt the land should remain the property of the former owners and they be allowed time to erect housing of a similar nature to that destroyed. It was pointed out that the single storey huts took up more area than a house and could only accommodate four persons. Foremost in the opposition to the encroaching pre-fabs was Mr E.D.K. Hall of Moyser Road, who campaigned long and vigorously against the "legalised robbers", even advocating a vigilante group to pull down any Portals being erected on bomb sites.

The builders of Streatham were less strident but felt the right way was to wait a few extra months and rebuild houses with bricks and mortar and reinstate the sites as before. This would be good for trade and give employment. It was to take a long while.

The call for more housing was to exercise the attention of all the candidates in the July 1945 General Election, as they were questioned repeatedly on their intentions by residents. Always a Tory stronghold, David Robertson was elected with a majority of 6000, a deservedly popular choice with his commitment to the people of Streatham during the war. In the House he championed the cause for homes, complaining in July 1946 that not a single permanent house had been built in Streatham. The foundations of two were started but abandoned for want of bricks.

By mid-1946 the Wandsworth Borough Rehousing Officer was re-establishing some 70 families a week. The Government had made an earlier plea for residents to offer vacant rooms for the homeless. Even with the incentive of the Council paying for the installation of separate cooking facilities met with poor response: in the first month of the scheme only four offers were received. Meanwhile many thousands of people were in need of homes since they were still occupying public shelters and rat-infested basements of ruins.

Aerial views of Streatham taken in July 1949 show clusters of pre-fabs on nearly all of the devastated areas. Over 400 were built. But during the 1950s the country's economy was freeing itself from the crippling war debt and the concrete huts were replaced by houses and blocks of flats. Few pre-fabs were to remain, with the last ones in Streatham being demolished in Christchurch Road in the mid-1980s.

After fifty years the scars of war have been all but swallowed up by rebuilding. Post-war social change has generated a mobile population which has scattered the folk memories of those dark days, soon to fade into oblivion as the survivors slip away. These pages of history are to establish a reminder and a record for future generations of the time when the courageous population of Streatham stood together to face its most perilous period and together rebuilt its community.

One of the last pre-fabs in Christchurch Road in the mid-1980s

Select Bibliography

Norman Longmate:

    The Doodlebugs   Hutchinson & Co., London, 1981

James McGovern:

    Crossbow & Overcast   Hutchinson & Co., London, 1965

Bob Ogley:

    Doodlebugs and Rockets

            Froglets Publications Ltd, Westerham, 1992

Rev. Canon D.M. Salmon:

    To, For, and About You - The People of Streatham

            St.Leonard's Church, Streatham, 1945

Richard Anthony Young:

    The Flying Bomb   Sky Books Press, New York, 1978

Croydon Advertiser:

    Courageous Croydon   *c.*1984

    The Streatham News   1944 and 1945

The First Edition of *Streatham's 41*

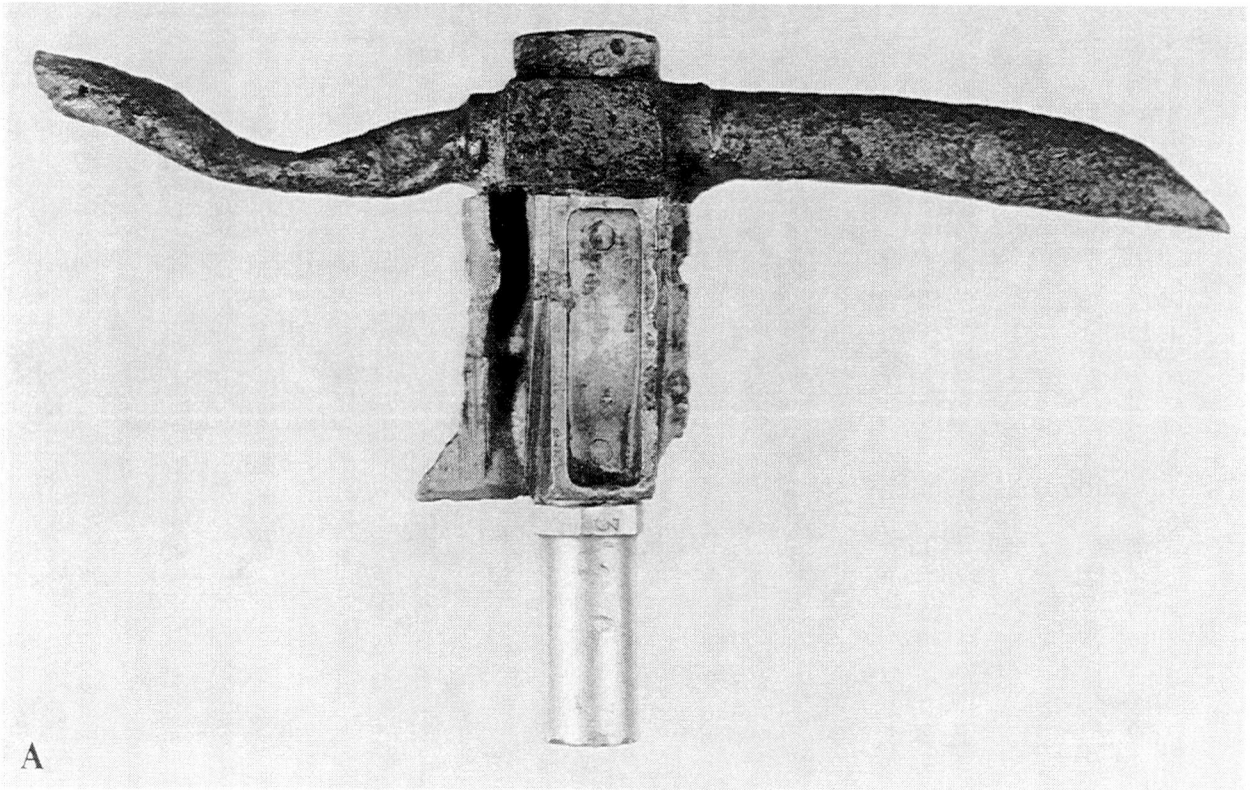

A: Vapourising Nozzle
found at Sunnyhill School

B: Windmill for Range Control
found on Streatham Common

C: Part of Pneumatic Servo Motor
found on Streatham Common

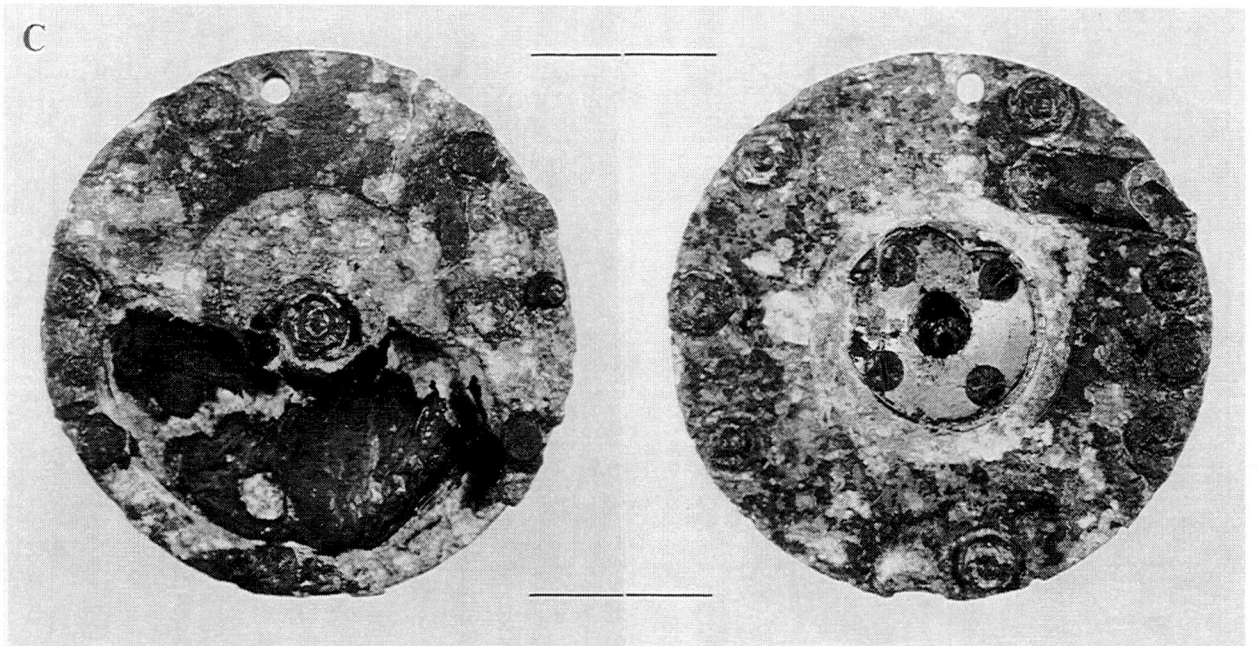

Examples of material found by metal detector
(same size)

24

Recovering V-1 Fragments

Colin Crocker

Metal detectors were developed from wartime portable mine-detecting apparatus. During the 1960s they were introduced to locate the presence of archaeological sites but have since come more popular as a leisure tool. Basically, the apparatus consist of a plate mounted at the end of a long handle which generates an electro-magnetic field. The proximity of metal (both ferrous and non-ferrous) will distort the field and modify the signal heard through headphones. It can locate metal objects to a depth of 6" - 12" and is ideal for pin-pointing hidden objects just beneath the soil surface.

I purchased a metal detector in 1976 and although it is known that the authorities at the time of the flying bombs collected as much as possible of these weapons for analysis, I set about searching on the various sites in the hope of finding overlooked fragments. The areas I have concentrated on are at Sunnyhill Road School (Bomb 11) and Streatham Common (Bombs 23 & 27). Since the explosions the sites have been used as allotments, so years of digging will have displaced the fragments. However, I have endeavoured to plot fragments as accurately as possible, working systematically within marked-out tracts. Each find is given a unique number and plotted onto a master plan of the site. The object is dug out by cutting through the turf on three sides of a square and hinging back. After removal of the object causing the signal, the sod is returned so that the grass surface is not damaged. Because of the disturbed nature of the sites and the method by which the objects were scattered, there is no "stratigraphy" associated with them, nor of any earlier deposited artefacts that might be chanced upon. The finds are cleaned and identified where possible. It is instructive to note that the objects found early in my work were of better condition than pieces now being uncovered, suggesting that they would deteriorate beyond recognition if left there indefinitely. This work has therefore been of value in preserving these wartime fragments.

To date I have managed to unearth 150 fragments. I do not have them positively identified in every case as being parts of flying bomb but I am fairly certain they are. I am grateful to the Imperial War Museum for their assistance in helping to identify these fragments.

My search for vestiges of the Sunnyhill Road School bomb started on 13th October 1979 (35 years after the bomb fell) and finished on 21st April 1984, 4½ years in all. The actual time spent on the searching over this period was 171 hours 30 minutes. By coincidence, the number of fragments found was 41 - the same number as bombs which fell on Streatham. I found the very first fragment within minutes of starting, although it was small enough to put in a matchbox. Other pieces were larger, such as a wing panel found some six months later. Another interesting portion was part of a vaporising nozzle. Some pieces still retained a coating of grey paint.

My search on Streatham Common has brought to light more fragments, the most easily identifiable was the propeller range-controller. It is a near miracle that this small item survived the blast being so close to the warhead. Other pieces have included a servo motor wheel and a component plate.

It is important that these fragments of history are brought to the surface and preserved before they are lost forever. Readers of this book, living on a former site of a V-1, who find strange pieces of twisted metal are requested to examine them carefully before discarding them. It could be part of "your" bomb! The Streatham Society would be interested in looking at it and retaining to add to the collection which will hopefully form a local museum where such pieces of the past could be made available for future generations.

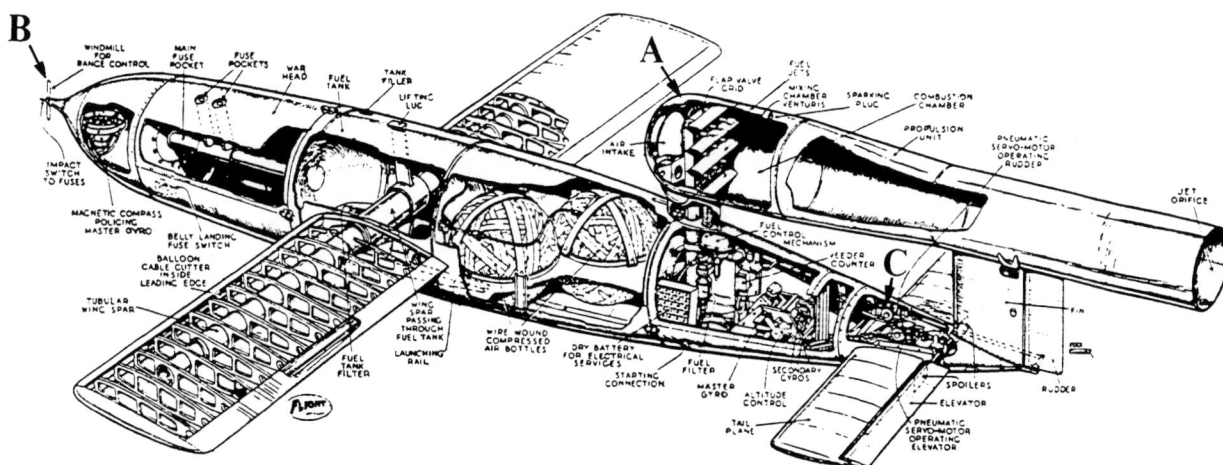

V-1 showing position of illustrated found items
(Reproduced with permission of *Flight International*)

Where the bombs landed

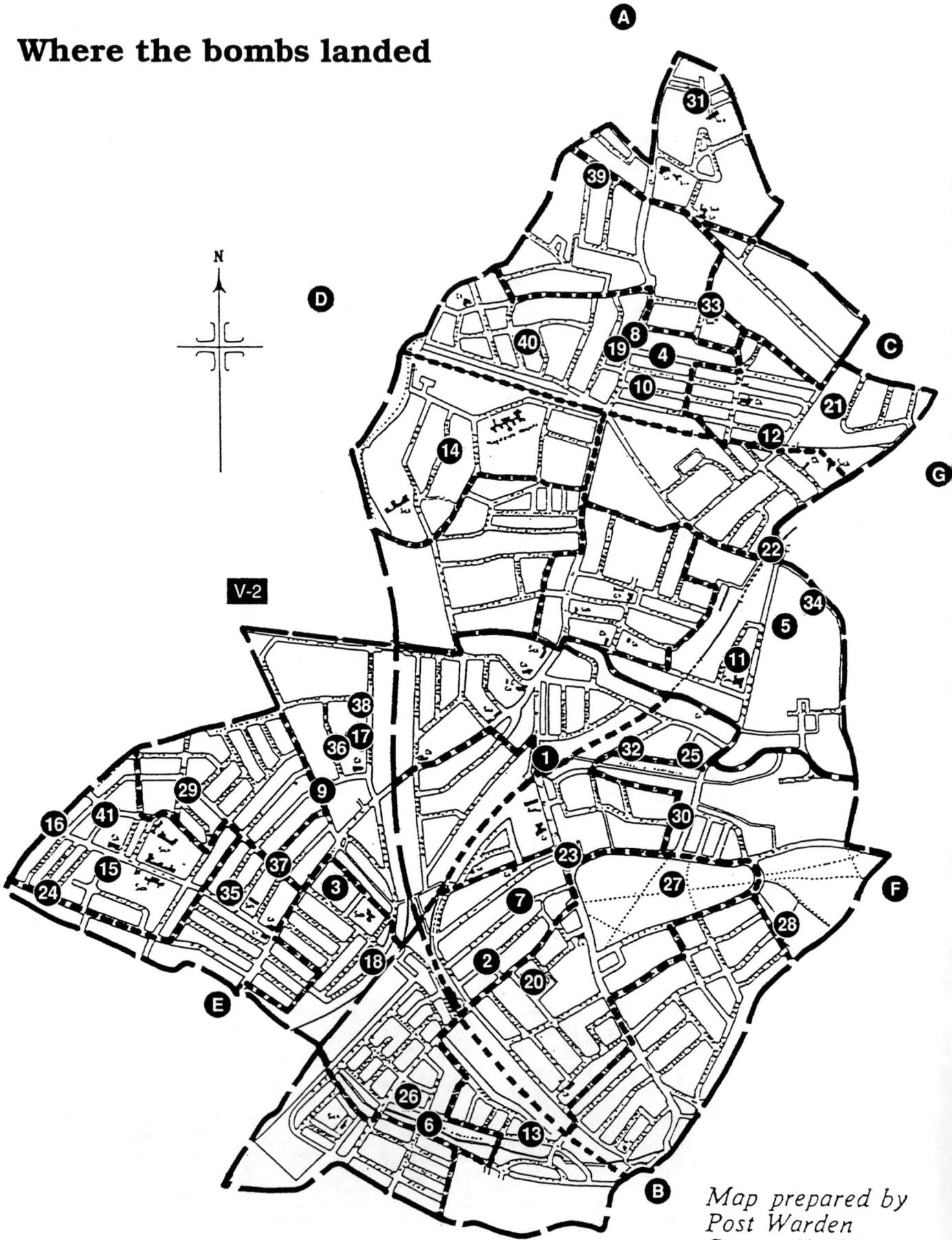

V-2

N

Map prepared by
Post Warden
Savoie K—93.

Streatham's 41 Flying Bombs

No.	Date	Time	Site	Post	No. deaths
1	June 16th	2 a.m.	Empire Cinema, Streatham High Road	J.90	0
2	June 18th	12-1 a.m.	23 Pathfield Road	J.87	3
3	June 18th	12-1 a.m.	25 Penrith Street	I.78	3
4	June 18th	12-1 a.m.	39 Downton Avenue	K.97	5
5	June 22nd		United Dairies, Valley Road	K.92	0
6	June 22nd	c.6 p.m	48 Sherwood Avenue	J.84	10
7	June 23rd	7 a.m.	75/77 Barrow Road	J.87	0
8	June 24th	12 midnight	Wyatt Park Mansions, Streatham Hill	K.97	0
9	June 26th	4 p.m.	Thrale Road	I.81	7
10	June 28th	1 a.m.	24/26 Barcombe Avenue	K.97	5
11	June 29th	8 a.m.	Sunnyhill Road School	K.92	0
12	June 29th	noon	205/17 & 256/68 Amesbury Ave	K.98	5
13	June 29th	7 p.m.	Sherwood Avenue/Glenister Park Road	J.83	0
14	June 30th	10.30 a.m.	11 Hoadly Road	K.95	1
15	July 1st	afternoon	34/36 Freshwater Road	I.79	2
16	July 1st	afternoon	47 Rectory Lane	I.79	3
17	July 1st	p.m.	19 Aldrington Road	I.81	0
18	July 3rd	5 a.m.	40 Besley Street	I.78	4
19	July 3rd	7 a.m.	Streatham Hill Theatre	K.97	1
20	July 3rd		Buckleigh Road	J.86	0
21	July 3rd	6.30 p.m.	93 Kingsmead Road	K.100	0
22	July 5th	1 a.m.	1a/1b Leigham Vale	K.96	2
23	July 5th	afternoon	War Memorial, Streatham Common	J.98	1
24	July 6th	8 a.m.	37 Southcroft Road	I.79	5
25	July 8th	late p.m.	9 Oakdale Road	J.89	7
26	July 10th	afternoon	Sherwood Avenue	J.84	0
27	July 13th	evening	Streatham Common	J.86	0
28	July 18th		Covington Way	J.91	0
29	July 21st	5 a.m.	144 Moyser Road	I.80	1
30	July 21st	evening	131 Hopton Road/Valley Road	J.91	1
31	July 22nd	6.10 a.m.	Lutheran Place	K.101	2
32	July 23rd	early a.m.	St.Anselm's Church, Madeira Road	J.89	4
33	July 27th	midnight	Wavertree Road/Daysbrook Road	K.100	1
34	August 1st	7 a.m.	150 Leigham Court Road	K.92	0
35	August 3rd	3 a.m.	Pendle Road	I.77	12
36	August 3rd		14 Abbotsleigh Road	I.81	0
37	August 5th		Moyser Road	I.80	2
38	August 6th		Aldrington Road	I.81	0
39	August 9th	6.45 a.m.	Tieney Road	K.99	0
40	August 13th	a.m.	3 Bellasis Avenue	K.97	0
41	August 13th	a.m.	132/134 Crowborough Road	I.79	0

Some Near Misses

	Date	Time	Site	Post	No. deaths
A	June 18th		Lyham Road	.33	
B	June 20th		Hermitage Bridge, Norbury		
C	June 22nd	5.09	53/59 Lanercost Road	.42	6
D	July 1st		near 14 Emmanuel Road	H.75	
E	July 3rd		"Mitcham"		
F	August 6th	6 a.m.	Ryecroft Road	.47	0
G	August 22nd	7.30 a.m.	Knollys Road	.45	1
V2	November 5th		Tooting Bec Common		0

Fatal Victims of V-1 Bombing on Streatham

Information mainly derived from the
Commonwealth War Graves Commission Civilian War Dead Roll of Honour

NAME	AGE	PLACE OF DEATH	INCIDENT
ALDEN, Donald P.	23	17 Furzedown Drive	Bomb 29
ALDEN, Muriel Janette	24	17 Furzedown Drive	Bomb 29
ALLSUP, Kate	67	22 Pathfield Road	Bomb 2
ALMOND, Elizabeth Duncan	52	"street"	Bomb 9
BARTON, Alice	75	41 Southcroft Road	Bomb 24
BARTON, Dora Evelyn	43	41 Southcroft Road	Bomb 24
BEGAS (?)		260 Amesbury Avenue	Bomb 12
BELLWOOD, Emma	63	"street"	Bomb 9
BIRD, Richard	70	31 Woodmansterne Road	Bomb 6
BRIDGE, Phyllis Maud	27	24 Barcombe Avenue	Bomb 10
BROWN, Douglas Albert	45	21 Oakdale Road	Bomb 25
BUNGAY, Arthur Theodore	71	26 Barcombe Avenue	Bomb 10
BUNGAY, Eliza	67	26 Barcombe Avenue	Bomb 10
BURT, Edward Droughton	71	39 Downton Avenue	Bomb 4
BURT, Harriet	65	39 Downton Avenue	Bomb 4
CLARKE, Clarence Henry	39	37 Downton Avenue	Bomb 4
COLLS, Alice Amlia Mary	69	9 Oakdale Road	Bomb 25
COMBAULT, Marguerite Leonie	70	121 Pendle Road	Bomb 35
CORBEN, Frank Henry	53	36 Moyser Road	Bomb 37
COX, Ellen	54	117 Pendle Road	Bomb 35
DANN, Irene Helena Margaret	25	20 Barcombe Avenue	Bomb 10
DAVIES, David Evan	59	50 Sherwood Avenue	Bomb 6
DEMMEN, John Kenneth	13	"street"	Bomb 16
DORRELL, Albert George	32	122 Pretoria Road	Bomb 35
DUNNING, Dorothy Renée	23	street o/s 31 Oakdale Road	Bomb 25
EDWARDS, Walter Herbert	77	21 Blegborough Road	Bomb 3
ELLIOTT, Frank	58	36 Besley Street	Bomb 18
FIASSIN, Josephine Louise	63	121 Pendle Road	Bomb 35
FORD, Alfred Samuel	72	117 Pendle Road	Bomb 35
FOX, Francis Edward	22	15 Madeira Road	Bomb 32
GARLAND, George Frederick	67	131 Hopton Road	Bomb 30
GITTUSS, Kate	72	119 Pendle Road	Bomb 35
GLADWIN, Bertram	56	41 Downton Avenue	Bomb 4
GLADWIN, Maud Mary	50	41 Downton Avenue	Bomb 4
HALL, Daniel	65	96 Southcroft Road	Bomb 24
HANCOCK, Mary	60	24 Barcombe Avenue	Bomb 10
HOWES, Martha	76	119 Pendle Road	Bomb 35
HUSSEY, Harriet	59	10 Oakdale Road	Bomb 25
HUTCHERSON, Alfred Charles	29	46 Sherwood Avenue	Bomb 6
HUTCHERSON, Doris Hilda May	25	46 Sherwood Avenue	Bomb 6
HUTCHINSON, Arthur William John	29	"street"	Bomb 9
HUTCHINSON, Gladys Alice Mary	30	"street"	Bomb 9
HUTCHINSON, Pauline Ann	1	"street"	Bomb 9
HYETT, Charlotte Anne	64	46 Sherwood Avenue	Bomb 6
JEFFERSON, William Henry	65	21 Penrith Street	Bomb 3
JONES, Emma Dorcas	88	Streatham Hill Theatre	Bomb 19
KERBEY, Charles Eli	84	23 Wavertree Road	Bomb 33
LAURENT, Helene	53	121 Pendle Road	Bomb 35
LAURENT, Martha	76	121 Pendle Road	Bomb 35
LEMEL, Laurie Eugenie	60	1 Oakdale Road	Bomb 32
LEMEL, Nathan	73	1 Oakdale Road	Bomb 32
LINDERS, Ann Catherina Josephina	4	260 Amesbury Avenue	Bomb 12
LINDERS, Joseph Anthonius	3	260 Amesbury Avenue	Bomb 12
LINDERS, Mary Matilda	42	260 Amesbury Avenue	Bomb 12
LINDERS, Stephen Joseph	2	260 Amesbury Avenue	Bomb 12

NAME	AGE	PLACE OF DEATH	INCIDENT
MACK, Jane Ann	77	10 Oakdale Road	Bomb 25
MACK, Robert Frederick	79	10 Oakdale Road	Bomb 25
McSWEENEY, Miss		11 Hoadly Road	Bomb 14
MANTON, George Edward	43		Bomb 16
MORGAN, Frederick Richard	59	29 Woodmansterne Road	Bomb 6
MORGAN, Olive Emily	48	29 Woodmansterne Road	Bomb 6
NECHAMKIN, Sophie	64		Bomb 9
PALMER, Thomas Gordon	45	123 Pendle Road	Bomb 35
POTTS, Annie Elizabeth	57	23 Pathfield Road	Bomb 2
POTTS, Violet Mary	59	23 Pathfield Road	Bomb 2
QUILLEN, Jeanne Rose	56	121 Pendle Road	Bomb 35
RAMSON, Alice Maud	68	30 Moyser Road	Bomb 37
RICE, Peter	10	22 Oakdale Road	Bomb 25
RICHARDSON, Cardine	85	119 Pendle Road	Bomb 35
ROBINSON, Stanley	30	27 Penrith Street	Bomb 3
RODFORD, Laura	80	1 Oakdale Road	Bomb 32
RUSSELL, Eric John	13	"street"	Bomb 24
RUSSELL, Francis Walter	36	1d Leigham Vale	Bomb 22
RUSSELL, John Richard Henry	7	1d Leigham Vale	Bomb 22
SALES, Daisy Margaret	68	19 Lutheran Place	Bomb 31
SALES, George Leonard	69	19 Lutheran Place	Bomb 31
SANDROFF, Florence Agnes	45	48 Sherwood Avenue	Bomb 6
SEARLE, Arthur John Thomas	57	Chinese Club	Bomb 23
SIMMONS, Gertrude	56	50 Rectory Lane	Bomb 16
STEVENSON, Ada Mary	28	27 Woodmansterne Road	Bomb 6
TROKE, Winifred Marguerite	48	39 Southcroft Road	Bomb 24
UNDERWOOD, Leonard Frederick	36		Bomb 9
WALLER, John Douglas	16	27 Woodmansterne Road	Bomb 6
WOOD, Beryl Olive	11	40 Besley Street	Bomb 18
WOOD, Charles Edward Horace Cecil	45	40 Besley Street	Bomb 18
WOOD, Edith Harriett	53	40 Besley Street	Bomb 18

Total Streatham Casualties

Killed	86
Seriously injured	335
Slightly injured	567
	988

Gold Wound Stripes
issued to A.R.P. wardens injured by enemy action which incapacitated them for at least 7 days

- Bell	I.78	Bomb 3
- Stoner	I.81	
- Jarvis	J.83	? Bomb 13
- Edward	J.85	
- Scott	J.85	
Egbert Kidby	K.92	Bomb 11
Mrs Cunningham	K.96	? Bomb 22
Jens Hansen	K.97	Bomb 40
John Sumner	K.98	Bomb 12
Miss Cantle	K.100	

Excerpts from the Wartime Diary of Mrs Gertrude Bathurst

99 Penwortham Road, Streatham, SW16

(Reproduced with kind permission of her son, Eric Bathurst)

June 15th 1944

These dreadful pilotless planes have started their destruction. Although we have longed for rain to improve the crops, we very much dislike it when it means bad visibility for the R.A.F. to see these little brutes. It don't know whether it is true but folk say Streatham is getting it worse than most places. I do know it is pretty bad.

June 18th

There is a dreadful mess the further side of Mitcham Lane (**Bomb 3**), four streets without a person living in them, every window, door and roof gone. All the roofs and windows in Mitcham Lane from Moyser Road to Thrale Road. We do not know how many casualties. I had a W.V.S. member call to make enquiries about bedrooms, there are 400 homeless and that number will soon increase if this bombing lasts. No Sunday Schools are being held, it is better to keep the children scattered, also all church halls and large empty houses are being taken over for storing the furniture of bombed-out families. We had to take shelter four times during breakfast. Of course, that is only three minutes each time but sometimes the engine stops and the plane travels a long way before dropping and other times the things burst in the air without the engine stopping. There is not a street without heaps of broken window glass and most houses have a pile of ceiling plaster in the gutter waiting for the lorry to fetch it away. Last Monday two doctors' houses in Thrale Road were demolished (**9**), the inmates were in shelters, but 5 adults and 1 child in the street were killed by blast. All up the High Road places on both sides are flattened. The Theatre will be unusable for six months (**8**).

July 1st

This has been a bad day for us, Welham, Freshwater, Remuir and Aldrington Roads, St.Paul's Church in Welham Road is not usable, neither is St.Alban's in Aldrington Road (**15-17**). The poor people in the College Hostel had a nasty shaking, they are all old or infirm and have been blitzed out of their homes in the East End. We know a dozen families personally who are either in hospital, killed or homeless; it makes one feel very sad and helpless.

July 3rd

This morning Douglas went to see if he could help at Besley Street, 5.30 a.m. (**18**). He says it is in an awful state.

[July 6th]

At 7.50 a.m. there was another crash, that one was in Southcroft Road (**24**),

I wonder how many people were killed. It has been raining incessantly which must have ruined a tremendous lot of homes where the roofs are stripped. Mrs Locke has evacuated as her house is blasted, so poor old Jim has to be charlady as well as everything else. He worries about me being alone when he is out on his round and I am very pleased to see him come home to see he is alright. I see there is a notice at the schools asking parents to evacuate their children, they only have to apply to the proper quarters and the children will be sent at once.

July 10th

All the stations are crowded with people trying to get away and crowds of children with their teachers. I get so tired of being indoors so Jim pushed my chair as far as the end of the road, the siren sounded so we hurried back to our cupboard under the stairs, ten went over in five minutes but none dropped near. Last night I laid and counted 51 bangs, some near and some far away.

July [?]12th

This morning about 8 o'clock one fell in Rural Way and 8 people were killed and in the night nearly every Council house at the end of Moyser Road was down (**29**). Poor Don [Alden] and Muriel MacKay were killed, they were only married in January and he was home on leave. We are certainly getting our share in this neighbourhood.

July 30th

Eric and Betty arrived this afternoon, he is on embarkation leave. They had little idea what buzz-bombs were like or what damage they did. They quite thought it would be possible to go to the City and the pictures but changed their mind by next morning. At 2.45 a.m. there was an awful crash the other side of the playground, one had fallen in the back gardens of Pretoria Road (**35**), it seemed as the noise of falling houses would never stop. All our windows, curtains, doors, walls and ceilings seemed to be falling. Glass was everywhere, sticking into the furniture, piano and tall-boy and also under the Morrison shelter where Betty and I both managed to get slightly cut. There were 17 people killed. Half an hour later another V-1 crossed straight over the house so low that it lit up the room. As soon as possible everybody got dressed and started clearing up, removing carpets and shaking them in the street. It was strange to see everyone doing the same thing all down the road. Betty said she thought

she would return home but Eric stayed to help clear up. Before she started off another one fell in Aldrington Road (**?36**). When they reached Paddington Station three more went over while they waited for the train.

[August 5th]

Saturday morning, and what a night we have had, they seem to have been coming over all the time, at 5 o'clock one fell at the corner of the road (**37**), just finishing off the rest of the ceilings and doors of all the houses in this street. All the places are ruined from this road to the next but I have not heard how many deaths. We had an army of sailors covering the windows on Thursday but now they have all to be done again. It is no exaggeration to say there are over a thousand houses with all the tiles off. We have no ceilings upstairs but only one partly down downstairs and the wall between the bedrooms blown through but poor Mrs Bone's place next door is in a dreadful mess. No doubt the school helped to shield us from the blast.

August [?]3rd

I am off to Wiltshire, we have managed to get a car to the station. When we left at 10 o'clock the street seemed almost impassable for tiles and glass. There were hundreds of sailors and Home Guard starting to cover the roofs with tarpaulins and doing windows. It made one feel sick. There were crowds of people waiting outside the barriers at Paddington but I and Jim were allowed through because the ambulance man had a chair for me. A few seats were reserved for folk like me so our journey was easy.

August 1944

You can guess I listened each morning to the wireless, although that did not give me much news about our district. After about three weeks Jim started to speak of crashes without any warnings in his letters but the papers and wireless did not give any information about [V-2] rockets. These dreadful things gradually increased in numbers and the buzz-bombs got less. I came back home in October expecting to find the house in a terrible mess as Jim had left the workman doing the landing ceiling, but our good fairy, Mrs Bone, had left her own muddle to make our place a bit tidy. We had several crashes much too close to be pleasant.

December 1944

Evidently we shall get no more repairs for many months to come. On the 28th the men started again in 97 but the snow was too thick for outside work.

Streatham's 41

The following maps show where the 41 Flying Bombs landed in Streatham in an attempt to place them in their geographical context. For the most part the annotations are from the original text of Kenneth Bryant's *Streatham's 41* of 1945, but to these have been added details no longer subject to censorship and subsequent information obtained by later research and reminiscences. Reminiscences are also interspersed between maps to add variety and to ensure appropriate facing pages.

The extent of bomb damage has been obtained from the L.C.C. Architects' maps of War Damage, presently deposited in the London Metropolitan Archives, 40 Northampton Avenue, London EC1. These do not distinguish between conventional bombing and individual flying bombs. The photographs come mainly from the original *Streatham's 41* with a few since uncovered.

With permission of the Ordnance Survey, the maps have been redrawn from the 60" series published prior to the war. Each map is to the same scale. The top of each page is north.

SCALE

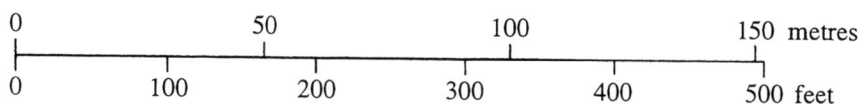

LEGEND

■	Totally destroyed	▨	Serious - repairable at cost
▨	Damaged beyond repair	▥	General blast
▨	Serious damage probably not repairable	▨	Blast damage
✦	V-1 hit	✧	H.E. bomb hit

⌂ Photograph taken looking in this direction

ABBREVIATIONS

A.A.	Anti-Aircraft (guns)	L.C.C.	London County Council
A.R.P.	Air Raid Precautions (p.5)	M.O.F.	Ministry of Food
A.T.C.	Air Training Corps	N.F.S.	National Fire Service (p.6)
A.T.S.	Auxiliary Territorial Service	P.W.	Post Warden (p.5)
C.D.	Civil Defence (p.5)	P.W.W.	Post Welfare Warden (p.5)
D.D.W.	Deputy District Warden (p.5)	R.A.F.	Royal Air Force
D.P.W.	Deputy Post Warden (p.5)	R.O.C.	Royal Observer Corps
D.W.	District Warden (p.5)	S.D.W.	Senior District Warden (p.5)
D.W.W.	District Welfare Warden (p.5)	S.W.	Senior Warden (p.5)
H.E.	High Explosive (of bomb)	V-1	*Vergeltungswaffe*-1 (p.7)
H.G.	Home Guard (p.7)	W.R.N.S.	Women's Royal Naval Service
I.I.P.	Incident Inquiry Post (p.6)	W.V.S.	Women's Voluntary Service (p.6)
I.O.	Incident Officer (p.5)	Y.M.C.A.	Young Men's Christian
L.A.C.	London Ambulance Corps		Association

Bomb 1

Streatham's first V-1 fell on the former Empire Cinema then being used as a food store. By the time the N.F.S. arrived, the heart of the store was 'going nicely', as Column Officer Williams put it. It was a tricky fire to fight for it was deep-seated and the firemen had to clamber up tottering mountains of tins and packing cases, with a very real danger of collapse into the fire. The smoke, too, made movement risky. Wardens were seen up aloft pointing a hose or shining torches to guide through the smoke.

The only occupant was the caretaker who was trapped under the debris, shocked but suffering only minor injuries. Two rescue workers extricated him seconds before the fire reached the spot where he had been pinned. An elderly man, he was quickly taken to the First Aid Post at the Baths, but in spite of the severe shaking and his wounds, would not rest until he had telephoned a report to his senior officer in the Ministry of Food. Total casualties were few.

A resident in a nearby house, who was in bed at the time, tells how hardly had the glass finished falling, when he heard a warden climbing the stairs calling out, "Stay where you are, I'm coming." Very glad he was to have followed this advice, for the warden's torch revealed a floor littered with broken glass - very menacing to bare feet.

Although this was mainly an 'N.F.S.' incident, the Streatham Welfare Scheme (a joint organisation of Wardens and W.V.S.) operating at its first fly bomb incident dealt excellently with over 120 persons requiring temporary shelter.

It is worthy of record that the Post Warden of J.90 put two wardens in charge who had only just completed their training as Incident Officers, and they came through very well.

The S.D.W. was seen carrying what looked like a piece of battered and perforated corrugated iron, but it proved to be part of the bomb complete with German lettering. This was hustled to headquarters by car and hustled back again a few hours later when the R.A.F. intelligence staff arrived in search of all possible clues, for little detail was known of these bombs at that time.

The Chief Warden inspected the scene early next day and Admiral Sir Edward Evans, one of London's Regional Commissioners, visited the incident about noon, accompanied by the Borough Controller, and was extremely interested in all he saw.

Full credit must be given to the N.F.S. and their salvage section, for by far the greater part of the food was saved and transported under M.O.F. supervision to other depots. Several wardens from various posts rallied round to an emergency call in the afternoon and helped form a human chain which loaded the lorries.

At the request of the police, the Home Guard took over the task of protecting the many damaged shops. They set about this in a thorough manner by throwing a line of men across the width of the High Road and advancing with rifles at the ready, challenging everybody. This had the effect of removing from the scene all unnecessary sightseers, and potential looters (if any). By mischance, some members of the Fire Guard were also eliminated (not liquidated) by this military manoeuvre, but that was "just one of those things." This guarding of damaged property is a rather dull and boring job for those doing it, but very much appreciated by the property owners, and the Home Guard helped the police frequently in this way.

One of the buildings severely damaged and rendered unusable was the Wesleyan Church. On the following day, it was scheduled to hold a Civic Service in connection with the Religion and Life Week, to be attended by His Worship the Mayor of Wandsworth. The service was transferred to St. Leonard's Church and duly held. The large congregation remained steady as a rock, whilst a flying bomb vibrated the very air as it passed right overhead to crash well within earshot, just over the boundary of a neighbouring division of the borough. It was to be another ten months before religious services could be resumed at the church - but only in the hall beneath.

A side-light of the flying bomb attacks was that they completely wrecked the follow-up work of the combined churches, which was proposed to take place subsequent to the Religion and Life Week, but the clergy found ample opportunity to contact the man and women-in-the-street and many of them rose to the occasion magnificently. During a particularly 'busy' spell, someone said it seemed that the "Religion and Life" Campaign had been followed by a period of "Devilry and Death".

A policeman guards the collected pieces of fly bomb

Bomb 1

Date: 16th June 1944
Time: 2 a.m.
Place: Empire Cinema, Streatham High Road
A.R.P. Post: J.90

Just before 2 a.m. eye-witnesses heard a roar like a low-flying plane followed by an explosion with a blinding flash and clouds of smoke. A shower of sparks rose from the spot where it landed covering the area with red-hot cinders. Debris, glass and tiles crashed all around.

The Weslyan Church was built in 1883. The bomb severely damaged the south transept and the organ was completely destroyed.

Numbers 7 and 9 were destroyed by H.E. bombs on 29th October 1940.

STANTHORPE   ROAD

The Bedford Park Inn and several shops and homes were damaged.

J.Charles, 225 Streatham High Road was a dyers and cleaners. It was completely wrecked by the blast, yet not a single garment was destroyed. They all required cleaning, of course.

The former Empire Cinema, built in 1910, closed in 1932, was used as an emergency food store. It was stacked high with tons of tea, sugar and tinned foodstuffs of all kinds. It took the full brunt of the explosion and quickly caught fire.

STREATHAM HIGH ROAD

Streatham Station

Total casualties were few and they were treated at the First Aid Post sited at the Swimming Baths.

The neighbouring railway line was blocked by debris, but soon after dawn this was cleared and trains ran normally. It was interesting to see lineswomen hard at it repairing the telephone lines, climbing the posts with quite professional skill.

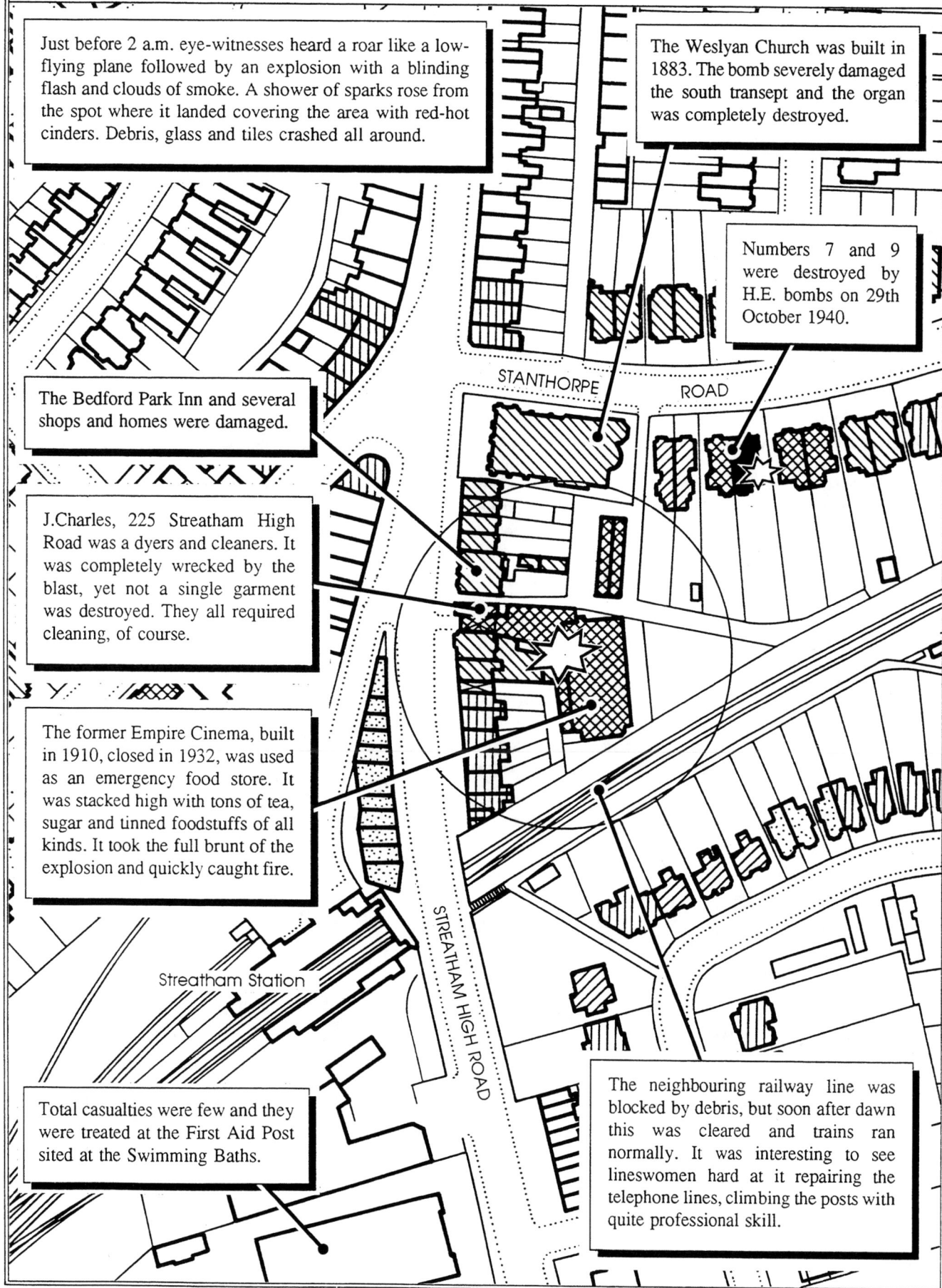

This map is based on the Ordnance Survey 60" map published in 1936

Bombs 2-4

Date: 18th June 1944
Time: Midnight - 1 a.m.
Place: various
A.R.P. Posts: J.87, I.78 & K.97

About 48 hours after the first, Streatham's fly bomb No.2 crashed in Pathfield Road (Post J.87). Fifteen minutes later No.3 fell in Penrith Street (Post I.78) and to complete the picture Downton Avenue (Post K.97) had No.4 only ten minutes after that. Here, indeed, was a situation to test Civil Defence to the limit, for all the bombs had fallen on residential areas and the blast damage was enormous; only comparable in previous experience with that caused by the land-mine which fell in the Vale during the 1940-41 blitz.

The number of houses reported damaged by these three flying bombs was just under 3,000. That night was pitch-dark and further bombs continued to roar over to the accompaniment of a terrific barrage from the ack-ack guns, and it was in these circumstances that Streatham's Civil Defence tackled their new problems. The ratio of casualties to material damage proved to be miraculously small, but this was not known at the time and until the house-to-house check-up had been completed, it was impossible for the respective Incident Officers to assess accurately just how much trouble they had to handle - but they did know it was plenty.

The Party Leaders prudently assumed that they would require considerable reinforcements. This meant that the lines of communication were crowded with urgent calls, and the Streatham telephone exchange certainly put up a grand show that night under very trying conditions. Divisional Office, for instance, had over 100 calls, and Borough Sub-Control, as the operational focus for two divisions must have had several times that number.

One important factor which emerged, and deserves full recognition, for its was common to all fly bomb incidents, was that the extent of damage inevitably involved the houses and homes of the very wardens who handled the incident. Time and time again, wardens reported for duty, having struggled out of a window or through a back garden because it was the only way of getting out from a wrecked home. Frequently, this involved leaving in trying circumstance (to put it mildly) a wife, aged parents or even children, but never once did the wardens in any area fail to rise to the occasion, putting the needs of others before their own misfortunes.

Here, perhaps, it is opportune to record the outstanding success of the automatic reinforcement scheme laid on by the District Wardens a few weeks before the attacks commenced. Many an I.O., short of personnel for the dozens of jobs he had to fill, had cause to thank the foresight shown and the generous way in which all posts operated the scheme to help their stricken neighbours.

Following the close of the Bomb 2 incident, a contact warden stands by on the scene to direct enquiries and post-raid services.

Bomb 2

Date: 18th June 1944
Time: night.
Place: 23 Pathfield Road
A.R.P. Post: J.87

Streatham's second fly bomb fell on Pathfield Road. D.P.W.Harrison acted as I.O., with support from the Post Warden and two Deputy District Wardens. The casualties were about 40 including some deaths.

Mrs Sheppard, a member of the W.V.S. and the wife of the Deputy District Warden, did good work by taking hot drinks to the working parties, notwithstanding the fact that her house was badly damaged. The rather long gap before the arrival of the mobile canteen which occurred on this occasion made her efforts doubly welcome. It is said that the Borough Controller, who visited the incidents during the night, himself went seeking the keyholder of the stores, whose safety measures were so good that the mobile canteens could get no supplies. Needless to say, no hold-up occurred subsequently.

Sisters Annie and Violet Potts died when the bomb hit their house at 23 Pathfield Road.

BARROW ROAD

PATHFIELD ROAD

Kate Allsup of 22 Pathfield died later in Wilson Hospital.

Heavy Rescue Party Leader Slater took abnormal risks in the operation, by working for some time in a position overhung by a very dangerous wall and displayed a quality of leadership worthy of high praise.

The care of the homeless was in the excellent hands of D.W.W. Henry Faulkner. Many of them were temporarily sheltered in the trenches on the Common and it proved possible to send a Y.M.C.A. canteen there to provide tea before they made the journey to the Rest Centre or other accommodation.

Streatham Common Station

This map is based on the Ordnance Survey 60" map published in 1936

Bomb 3

Date: 18th June 1944
Time: night.
Place: 25 Penrith Road
A.R.P. Post: I.78

This fly bomb was almost certainly the most damaging of Streatham's 41, for it affected no less than 1,671 houses.

Eye witness, William Page, was standing on the corner of Blegborough Road when he saw a rocket from the Tooting Common A.A. unit hit the bomb's wing causing it to crash. By cruel coincidence, the daughter of some of the casualties was in the A.T.S. working with the battery.

The I.O. was D.P.W. Ernest Long, who had only completed his course and exam three days before, but handled a trying task very well indeed. He received full backing from Mr Waight, then "Acting" "I" District Warden, who was on the scene very quickly, also from the Post Warden and, indeed, all wardens of I.78 and other posts, who rallied round.

Walter Edwards died at 21 Blegborough Road.

William Jefferson of No.21 died later in St.James' Hospital.

Fire guard Stanley Robinson died when his house at 27 Penrith Street collapsed.

Warden Bell, although he received a fractured arm and face wounds from his dented helmet, assisted in rescue work and other duties until forced to go to hospital the following day.
Warden Johnson was only slightly less commendable, carrying on despite severe blasting.

Several H.E. bombs fell in the area on 16th October 1940.

A contingent of Tooting Home Guard (the whole of "I" District was in their area) gave valuable aid on Sunday morning in debris clearance and the continuing search for missing persons.

A particularly striking feature was that warden "first aiders" dealt with 150 slightly injured persons in the adjoining Rest Centre. Miss Windridge was one of those wardens and received congratulations from a doctor for the standard of her work. Known affectionately as "Windy" - a most inappropriate nickname - she was to be seen at most "I" District incidents with her first-aid kit.

BLEGBOROUGH ROAD

PENRITH STREET

FERNTHORPE ROAD

CUNLIFFE STREET

This map is based on the Ordnance Survey 60" map published in 1936

Bomb 4

Date: 18th June 1944
Time: night.
Place: 39 Downton Avenue
A.R.P. Post: K.97

The third flying bomb of the night landed in Downton Avenue, wrecking many wardens' homes. Notwithstanding this, and the newness of the problems created by these weapons, it was not long before D.P.W. Arthur Neal had taken over as I.O. and established effective control. The services arrived quickly and some fine work was carried out. The "K" District Warden and his deputies gave constant support to the I.O. throughout the night.

Edward and Harriet Burt, an elderly couple, were killed when their house at 39 Downton received a direct hit.

An action station received a direct hit. Warden Bertram Gladwin had returned there after reporting at the post. He and his wife, Maud, who was a Fire Guard Street Party Leader, were apparently on their doorstep at number 41 when the bomb exploded. Their daughter was injured.

Fire Guard Clarence Clarke died at his home 37 Downton Avenue.

An H.E. bomb had landed in the back garden of 35 Cricklade on 25th October 1940 causing great damage and the death of Mabel Van der Weth at number 37.

DOWNTON AVENUE

CRICKLADE AVENUE

BARCOMBE AVENUE

There were plenty of homeless to be cared for, and D.W.W. Eustace Belham soon arrived and took over this work. Many were directed to a nearby hall, and from there removed to a rest centre by Green Line coaches. This was no pleasure trip with further fly bombs sailing overhead and incessant gunfire. L.A.C. Marks (ex Divisional Office), who was on leave, spent it helping, and amongst other jobs, rode on the bonnet of the coach to direct the driver.

Mrs Begg, a lady warden, was particularly commended by the Heavy Rescue Party for the cool and efficient way she carried out the tricky job of "Occupants' Checker" - her home, too, had been blasted.

It was 10 p.m. Sunday before this incident was closed, a long delay being caused by trying to find two persons who had gone away but not advised the wardens.

This map is based on the Ordnance Survey 60" map published in 1936

Bomb 4

Date: 18th June 1944
Time: night
Place: 39 Downton Avenue
A.R.P. Post: K.97

I was with the Glenn Players, an amateur dramatic group, which was presenting J.B. Priestley's *Dangerous Corner* at St.Mary's Hall, Clapham Common, on 17th June. A day or two later the performance would most certainly have been cancelled, but at this point in time, we went on.

The drone of the bombs was heard during the evening performance and the lines exchanged between Olwen and Freda were peculiarly apposite:

Olwen: This is quite mad, isn't it?

Freda: Quite mad, and rapidly getting madder.

We stayed the night in Basil's house, and when Jack took me home the next morning, we could hardly believe our eyes. The whole of Streatham Hill was littered with broken glass. Downton Avenue, they said, had got the worst of it. It had indeed.

Nora Gladwin, married to a soldier, was now living with her parents at 41 Downton Avenue. She had been in the audience for *Dangerous Corner*. In the small hours of the following morning, her parents' house was destroyed. Her father, an air-raid warden, who had been standing near the glass porch, was killed instantly; her mother died later in hospital. Nora was taken to the South London Hospital for Women at Clapham. It was said you could see the imprint of her hand in blood on her bedroom wall, which was exposed to the elements.

I visited Nora in hospital next day. Joan Marquardt came with me, and we were appalled when we saw Nora. She had not been a great beauty but she had a gentle, motherly face and it was now completely criss-crossed with black scars. Her many cuts had to be sewn up immediately without cleansing in order to prevent her bleeding to death. On top of this she had been painted with gentian violet which added to her bizarre appearance, and Joan - who had earlier warned me I must get a good grip on myself because I was so sensitive - took one look at her and fainted clean away.

"Oh, dear," said Nora, "I must look worse that I thought." A little later, when Joan had recovered, Nora said to me, "I did enjoy *Dangerous Corner* last night." I think at that moment, I *knew* we would win the War. Here was a girl who had lost her home, her parents and her looks and could still remark on how much she had enjoyed our play. How could a spirit like that be conquered?

from *Wartime Playtimes*
by Brenda Hargreaves

A reminiscence from
Alan Rolfe

I was living at 10 Wyatt Park Road when Downton Avenue was hit. I afterwards counted some 40 houses destroyed and another 100 damaged. I was particularly struck by the way glass from the windows had embedded itself in the opposite wall.

Workmen came next day to put plastic in the windows. The cellar had withstood the blast and I decided to sleep there. However, the water tank in the roof was ruptured and leaked down. When a warden came round to inquire of any problems, I replied I was having trouble with my water. The warden remarked he could not do anything about that. But the tank was fixed the next day. I was able to enjoy a bath with the starry sky as my ceiling, until tarpaulins for the roof came about a week later.

Tuesday, 20th June

The next damage was when Post J.85 got the blast from a very near-miss, which landed just over the Croydon (Norbury) boundary. Over 500 Streatham houses were damaged and the casualties included five wardens - fortunately none serious.

The Gladwins' funerals

The funeral of Warden Bertram Gladwin and his wife, who had been killed by the Downton Avenue bomb, took place at St.Margaret's Church, Barcombe Avenue, on the afternoon of Monday, 26th June. It was attended by many of his fellow wardens from K.97, led by Post Warden Lumley. The Senior District Warden, the Divisional Officer and Divisional Fire Guard were also present and several members of the W.V.S. Just as the service ended and the bearers rose to carry the coffins from the church, the rasping note of an approaching fly bomb was heard. The mourners remained quietly standing without a waver as the bomb roared overhead, to explode a mile or two further on. It was an impressive and tense moment which few present will ever forget.

Red Cross Cadets with a casualty they have just treated (Bomb 23)

Bomb 5

Date: 22nd June 1944
Time:
Place: United Dairies Field, Valley Road.
A.R.P. Post: K.92

The bomb fell within 50 feet of an electricity sub-station. One of the largest in England, with a capacity of 150 000 kva, it supplied not only Streatham but Wandsworth, Lambeth, Mitcham and many others areas. Although the control room was severely damaged, supply was restored to all consumers - over 200 000 - almost immediately.

K.92 got their first flying bomb, and although it fell on open ground, it made the usual nasty mess of the surrounding buildings in Valley Road. The I.O. was S.W. William Morley, only recently having sat the exam, and he discharged the responsibility very well.

A remarkable escape was that of a man inside a sand-bag enclosure only a few yards from the bomb when it exploded.

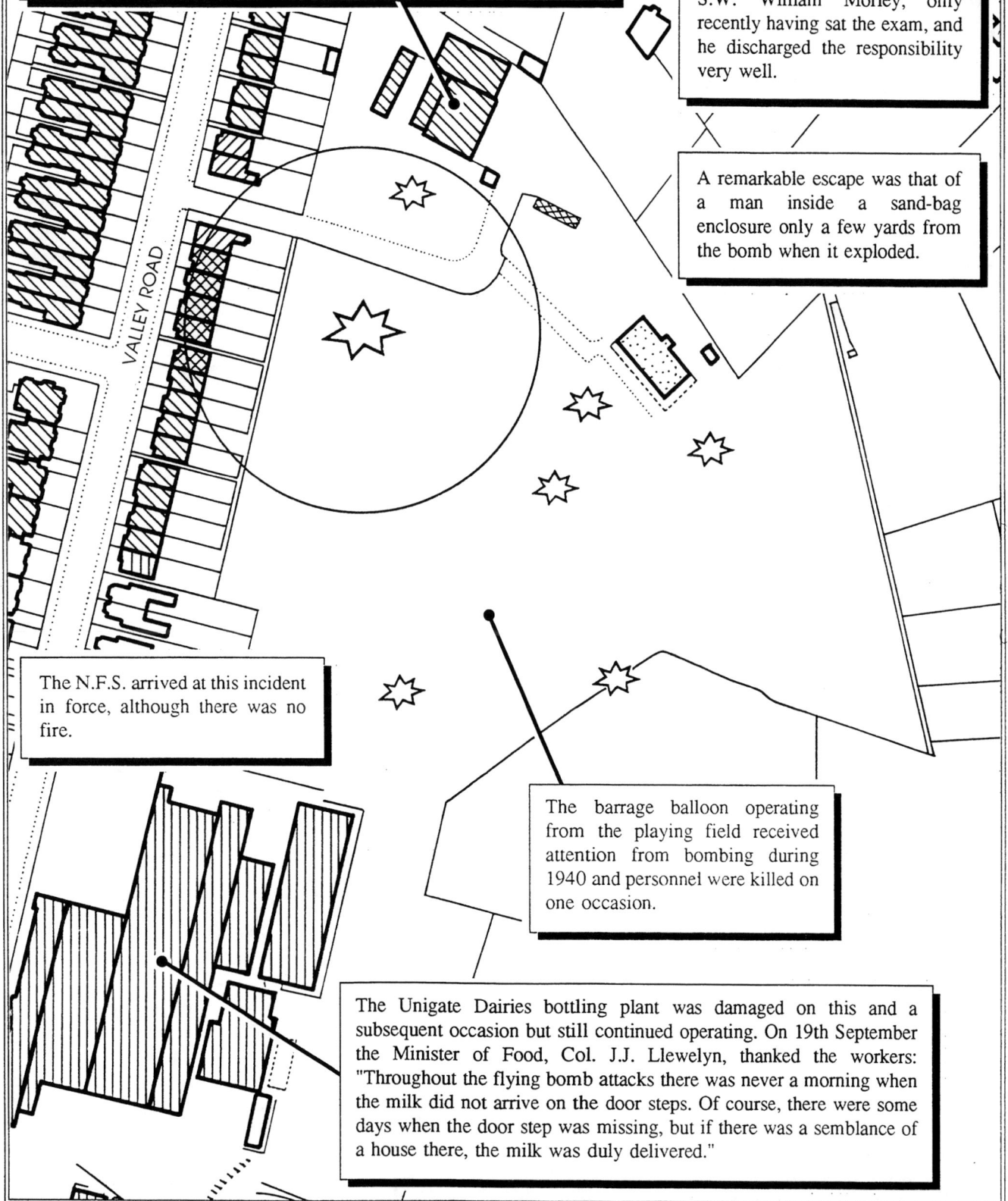

VALLEY ROAD

The N.F.S. arrived at this incident in force, although there was no fire.

The barrage balloon operating from the playing field received attention from bombing during 1940 and personnel were killed on one occasion.

The Unigate Dairies bottling plant was damaged on this and a subsequent occasion but still continued operating. On 19th September the Minister of Food, Col. J.J. Llewelyn, thanked the workers: "Throughout the flying bomb attacks there was never a morning when the milk did not arrive on the door steps. Of course, there were some days when the door step was missing, but if there was a semblance of a house there, the milk was duly delivered."

This map is based on the Ordnance Survey 60" maps published in 1935 and 1936

Bomb 6

Date: 22nd June 1944
Time: about 6 p.m.
Place: 48 Sherwood Avenue
A.R.P. Post: J.84

Streatham Vale had its first fly bomb which exploded in a culvert of the River Graveney which ran between the back gardens of Sherwood Avenue and Woodmansterne Road. Three roads were drastically affected and there were over 40 casualties. At that time in the evening large numbers of residents were returning from business and there were tragic home-comings for many.

With so much going on at the same time, and casualties being sent away from several points, it was no light task to keep track of them. Warden Pressdee as Loading Ground Warden tackled this job very efficiently.

Five people were killed in 46-50 Sherwood Avenue, including Alfred and Doris Hutcherson, married just two years.

A landmine had devastated 31-35 Drakewood Road on 16th April 1941.

A bomb hit 40 Drakewood Road on 15th October 1940.

Five people were killed at 27-31 Woodmansterne.

Warden Franklin Keightley acted as I.O., most ably assisted by Warden George Watt, who ran out of his chemist's shop at 99 Streatham Vale to help.
Any number of volunteer helpers set to work feverishly on rescue operations; services flooded in from Streatham and other Wandsworth Divisions, also from Mitcham and Croydon. The local Fire Guard were especially good, and many Home Guard helped.

The mobile canteen presented to Civil Defence by the residents and traders of Streatham was early on the scene, manned by Divisional Office staff, and proved a wonderful boon, as it did over and over again.

SHERWOOD AVENUE

DRAKEWO...

HELMSDALE ROAD

WOODMANSTERNE ROAD

This map is based on the Ordnance Survey 60" map published in 1940

Bomb 6

Date: 22nd June 1944
Time: about 6 p.m.
Place: 48 Sherwood Avenue
A.R.P. Post: J.84

As one would expect in the Vale, good neighbourliness and self-help were to be seen everywhere. P.W. William Thompson ably organised the removal of furniture from damaged houses and with the help of local firms' lorries and vans, plus those sent in by the Borough, this aspect of the job was completed by Sunday. The N.F.S. also gave great help in the post-raid clear-up both here and at many other incidents.

It also marked the first appearance in Streatham of a Ministry of Works' flying squad of workmen to tackle first-aid repairs.

The mobile canteen presented to Civil Defence by the residents and traders of Streatham was early on the scene, manned by Divisional Office staff, and proved a wonderful boon.

Another novelty was the attendance at mid-day Friday of a mobile bath unit consisting of hot shower-bath cubicles complete with towels and soap. The bathrooms of many houses had been rendered useless, so the opportunity to get rid of the ingrained dust and grime was most welcome.

There were quite a number of homeless to be sheltered. Some went to Eardley Road and Defoe Road Rest Centres, many were housed locally by friends, others were transferred by V.C.P. cars to more remote addresses. All this was fixed up by the Streatham Welfare Scheme. The warden side of this Organisation was represented by D.W.W. Faulkner and P.W.W. Lawrence, and the W.V.S. by Mrs Bailey, Mrs Thompson and many others. Mrs Nutting, Borough Organiser, also managed to get over from Wandsworth.

The V.C.P. cars were of immense assistance throughout the bombing in helping to get away old folks, invalids and others not able to use public transport. Mileage had to be watched carefully and on this occasion when a lady warden came into the Incident Inquiry Point saying she had two expectant mothers to be moved, the usual question was put "How far have they got to go?" The reply, however, was unexpected - "Well, one of them, 5 weeks."

Falling within a stone's throw of where a land mine fell in 1941, this flying bomb wrecked hundreds of homes. Note the undamaged mirror on the bedroom wall and the Anderson shelter in the foreground.

41

Bomb 7

Date: 23rd June 1944
Time: 7 a.m.
Place: 75/77 Barrow Road
A.R.P. Post: J.87

Just before 7 a.m. on the 23rd June a fly bomb crashed in Barrow Road. Pathfield, Lewin, Natal and surrounding roads were also badly blasted, many houses suffering damage for the second time in a week.

The heart of the incident consisted of four completely collapsed houses - 73-79 Barrow Road. Each presented a long job for the Rescue Services and the immediate problem was to decide where to work first - where were the trapped casualties?
The wardens gave the picture according to their Occupants' Cards (very recently checked) and neighbours helped, but nevertheless for two and a half hours a Rescue party aided by wardens, N.F.S., Home Guard and other volunteers, worked desperately shifting tons of debris, only to learn that the supposed casualty had been traced by the police to a South Coast town!

D.P.W.Harrison, of J.87, acted as Incident Officer and was warmly commended by his senior officers. The backing he received from wardens of J.87, J.86 and other posts was admirable. A.T.S. personnel voluntarily gave assistance shifting debris. The Vicar of Immanuel Church, Revd. Oscar de Berry, and his curate were untiring in their efforts to assist the elderly and homeless, whilst the Welfare Organisation was again right in the picture and, of course, the W.V.S. Incident Inquiry Point.

Lewin Road Baptist Church was severely blasted with its windows blown in. A renovation fund was started immediately. The first service held there afterwards was on 3rd September when the Rev. Angus McMillan preached on "Unshakable Foundations".

Barrow Road entered the war on the first day of the Blitz, 7th September 1940.

Whilst the Light and Heavy Rescue Leaders were completing their reconnaissance, a lady Fire Guard heard a faint cry in a certain part of the debris. Quickly this was confirmed and the plan of rescue laid down by the Heavy Rescue Leader. Doctor Lawson was present on this occasion.
This rescue was typical of the fine work performed during the attacks. With little more than an hour, verbal contact had been made by tunnelling towards the trapped casualty, who was a 17-year old girl. Oxygen was administered by tube and the Heavy Rescue Officers kept up a running conversation with her throughout the four hours the operation took. The casualty showed great spirit and when one arm was freed, asked for and received a wet flannel to wash her face. On learning the time, she jokingly said, "Oh dear, I shall be late - missed the workman's fare too. Never mind, I'll get the cheap mid-day rate on the trams." No, not rambling nor hysteria, just plain British pluck.

During the afternoon, Col. Llewellin, the Minister of Food, visited the scene and, amongst other points, was anxious to learn if the mobile canteens were giving satisfactory service.

This map is based on the Ordnance Survey 60" map published in 1936

Bomb 8

Date: 24th June 1944
Time: midnight.
Place: Wyatt Park Mansions, Streatham Hill.
A.R.P. Post: K.97

Wyatt Park Mansions, built in the mid-1930s, took a direct hit. The building stood it well and there was no collapse, hence few serious casualties. A second search was made in case any casualties had been overlooked. Whilst the N.F.S. were helping the wardens with this task, a lady rushed up to one of them, crying "My husband! Oh, my husband!!" Said the gallant fireman, "That'll be all right, madam - just tell us where he is and we'll get him out in no time." "He's up in the West End on fire watch," came the surprising answer.

A most acceptable form of help was provided by a military unit, who sent a bulldozer, which made short work of clearing the debris from the main road, thus aiding both the removal of casualties by ambulance and the police in restoring normal traffic, and at that time Streatham Hill was a vital through route for Second Front supplies.

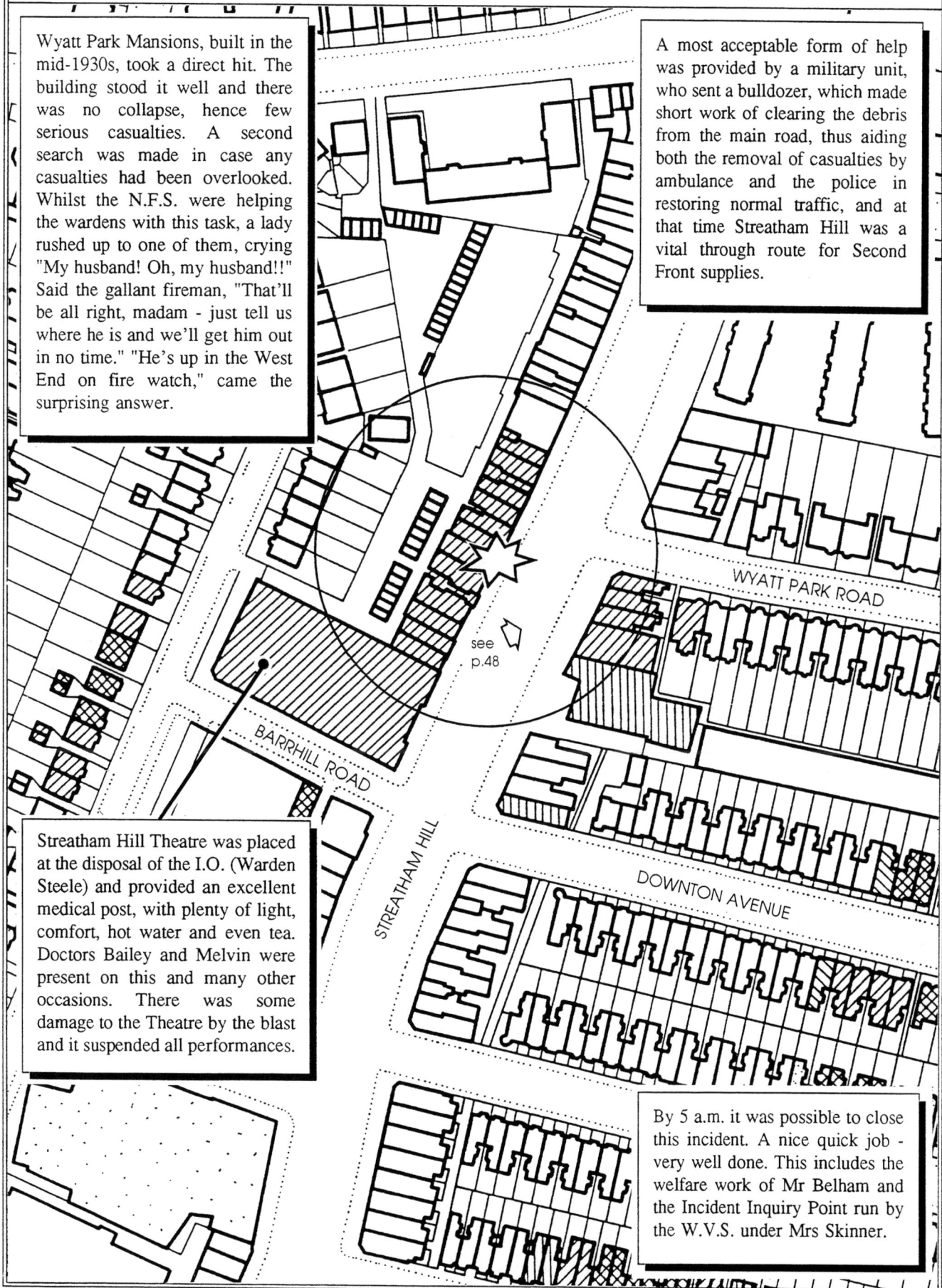

see p.48

WYATT PARK ROAD

BARRHILL ROAD

STREATHAM HILL

DOWNTON AVENUE

Streatham Hill Theatre was placed at the disposal of the I.O. (Warden Steele) and provided an excellent medical post, with plenty of light, comfort, hot water and even tea. Doctors Bailey and Melvin were present on this and many other occasions. There was some damage to the Theatre by the blast and it suspended all performances.

By 5 a.m. it was possible to close this incident. A nice quick job - very well done. This includes the welfare work of Mr Belham and the Incident Inquiry Point run by the W.V.S. under Mrs Skinner.

This map is based on the Ordnance Survey 60" map published in 1936

Bomb 9

Date: 26th June 1944
Time: 4 p.m.
Place: Thrale Road.
A.R.P. Post: I.81

The flying bomb fell in Thrale Road about 4 p.m. The services, including N.F.S., police and warden reinforcements from many posts, arrived promptly. The damage was extensive, 1000 houses being affected. Casualties numbered over 30.

A large tree had been blown down, blocking Fayland Avenue and heavy rain set in which made everything more difficult for the services and multiplied the hardship of those whose roofs had been lifted by the blast.

A lad pushing a handcart 25 yards from the bomb was among the injured. The cart was blown to fragments, but the lad was alive and after attention from a doctor was rushed by ambulance to hospital.

THRALE ROAD

FAYLAND AVENUE

D.D.W. Ames acted as I.O., with Miss Rippon as clerk. Lady wardens were naturally predominant (the men being mostly out of the area at work) and included Mrs Goldsworthy and Mrs Wagstaff (who did a splendid job of first aid), Mrs Braham, Mrs B.K.Smith and Miss Milnes, "I" District Welfare Warden. Head Fire Guard Turner and Senior Fire Guard Sainsbury gave valuable assistance.

There were six fatalities, all caught in the open. A young couple from nearby Gracedale Road, (the Hutchinsons) with their two year old daughter, were among them: "In death they were not divided" ran the *In Memorium*.

The house of Dr Morrish, 32 Thrale Road, caught fire but this was quickly brought under control by the N.F.S. He was trapped in the shelter and it took four hours to release him. Other doctors living in the road also had their homes damaged (Dr Keates at No.30 and Dr Wilkinson at No.26).

One especially paltry thing happened on this occasion. A casualty about to be removed to hospital was worried about the care of her dog. A woman standing by offered to look after it, but neither she nor the dog was seen afterwards. The owner on her recovery seemed more distressed by this than the loss of her home.

This map is based on the Ordnance Survey 60" map published in 1936

Bomb 10

Date: 28th June 1944
Time: 1 a.m.
Place: 24/26 Barcombe Avenue
A.R.P. Post: K.97

K.97 took its third knock within ten days when the bomb roared down the road at roof level landing on 24 Barcombe Avenue, killing two women.

Warden Henry Steele took charge as I.O. and was ably backed by the other wardens, including D.W.Garrett, with his deputies, T.J.Bryant and C.T.Hack. P.W. Evan Lumley concentrated on the lines of communication - a vital but non-spectacular side of incident procedure.

A nurse carried a child all the way from Barcombe Avenue to the first aid post at Brixton Hill and then walked back to minister to the minor casualties gathered in the Locarno.

Dr Bailey and Dr Margaret Melvin rendered excellent service, as they did at the previous two K.97 incidents (and many others). Dr Sinclair did a specially good job in climbing high into a dangerous structure to attend to a critically injured casualty before he could be moved.

At 20 Barcombe Avenue, young Irene Dann, married only three years and known as "Bunty" to her mother-in-law, was killed.

One man was found in bed with the ceiling open to the sky but he was rescued unharmed.

Although the bomb fell after 1 a.m., the Locarno Dance Hall was immediately opened by Robert Davis, the manager, as a temporary haven for the homeless and casualties. One of the people was a mother who had returned that very day from a nursing home with her fortnight-old baby. Over 1000 cups of tea were supplied during the night to those unfortunate people, also to the services and nearby shelters. D.W.W. Eustace Belham and P.W.W.Alexander collected the homeless and when daylight came, they were transported to Rest Centres, having been very comfortably accommodated in the meantime, thanks to the Locarno.

At 24 Barcombe Avenue, two women, Phyllis Bridge and Mary Hancock were killed.

At 26 Barcombe Avenue, an elderly married couple, Arthur and Eliza Bungay were killed.

A member of the N.F.S. bent his back under a broken water-pipe to protect a trapped casualty, and although totally soaked, stayed until the water was turned off.

STREATHAM HILL

BARCOMBE AVENUE

This map is based on the Ordnance Survey 60" map published in 1936

45

Bomb 11

Date: 29th June 1944
Time: 8 a.m.
Place: Sunnyhill Road School
A.R.P. Post: K.92

Just after 8 a.m. K.92 had its second flying bomb which fell in the gardens between Valley and Harborough Roads.
P.W. Alfred Brimicombe took charge, and with the help of wardens who willingly postponed their departure to business, soon established control.

There were no fatal casualties and only four needed to go to hospital. Two wardens, Egbert Kidby and his wife, Rose, were injured. Warden Kidby was later issued a gold wound stripe for injuries which caused incapacity for at least seven days. The sixty homeless were well cared for by P.W.W. Masters and Miss Pollock. The assistant Chief Warden (Mr H.W.Fray) visited this incident.

The bomb fell on soft ground so there was a sizeable crater, and some very interesting bits were found in it, all of which were taken over by the police.

Mrs Marshall lived at 57 Harborough Road; her reminiscence is opposite.

* Fragments of the V-1 were found by metal detector investigation in the 1980s.

Mrs Ritherdon lived at 172 Valley Road: her reminscence is opposite.

The pupils of Sunnyhill Road School had fortunately not arrived. Although the building was too damaged to allow teaching, in a couple of days arrangements were made to accommodate them elsewhere.

Months later, Mrs Cordrey of 180 Sunnyhill complained of wanting a home in which to receive her sons from Italy and a German P.O.W. camp. She had lost all she had and the remnants of her furniture were huddled in a corner of a room to keep them dry.

During the Victory celebrations, King George VI and Queen Elizabeth toured the suburbs. On 10th May 1945, they visited the School grounds with the Mayor of Wandsworth to inspect the local A.R.P. groups.

Post K.92 was in the School caretaker's house.

HARBOROUGH ROAD

VALLEY ROAD

This map is based on the Ordnance Survey 60" map published in 1936

Bomb 11

Date: 29th June 1944
Time: 8 a.m.
Place: Sunnyhill Road School
A.R.P. Post: K.92

A reminiscence from
Mrs Winifred Marshall
57 Harborough Road

It was a day of several near misses and she almost wished that one would hit her and end the suspense. The flying bomb took down the backs of hers and her neighbours' houses although the fronts were undamaged. There were two cats in the neighbourhood but one disappeared. There were also five chickens in a back yard: one went up and came down only as feathers, the four others came into the house and promptly laid eggs!

Mrs Marshall had her two children with her, a daughter aged 1 and a son aged 3. They were trapped in their Anderson shelter inside their home. The son lost his speech after the blast and when he did regain it after a year it was with a stutter. Whilst trapped, they heard footsteps but no-one came to rescue them. Afterwards they discovered their ration books were missing. In contrast, after Heavy Rescue released them, the men went round the site picking up loose stamps from the son's stamp collection. The daughter's clothes had been blown into a nearby tree. The wardrobe in the bedroom was sheared off to the bottom drawers. The family evacuated afterwards to Torquay.

A reminiscence from
Mrs Ritherdon
172 Valley Road

Mr Ritherdon worked with the Fire Service and lived away from home most of the time. Mrs Ritherdon lived in the downstairs maisonette with her son, Douglas, and her one year old daughter, Jill. Douglas slept in the Morrison shelter in the back room and at the sound of a siren, Mrs Ritherdon would run from her room clutching the baby and throw herself in with the son.

The threat, although new, soon prompted fear reactions and Mrs Ritherdon recalled her dash down Sunnyhill Road to the school shelters on hearing a V-1. Ten days after the start of the offensive, the family evacuated to friends in Hemel Hempstead. Her friends derided her for the fear she displayed at the sound of any approaching plane.

Two days after leaving Valley Road, a V-1 struck behind the School. The whole back of the house was demolished. The heavy Morrison shelter had been sucked across the room with the back draft from the explosion. When she returned home Mrs Ritherdon was distressed to find items stolen - some precious, some mundane, like the umbrella hanging in the hall. Much of the furniture was damaged but she was awarded compensation. The family was temporarily housed in one of the large houses facing Streatham Common. They lived there until they acquired No. 96 Valley Road, but when they arrived to take up residence there was still a foot of rubble on the site.

The Royal Visit to Sunnyhill School in May 1945 showing the damaged houses in Harborough Road.

Above: Parade of shops and flats along Streatham Hill opposite the blast at Wyatt Park Mansions, showing loss of roofs, glass windows and frontages. (Bomb 8)

Right: Damage at the top of Amesbury Avenue. Again, the bomb fell on houses on the other side of the road. (Bomb 12)

Bomb 12

Date: 29th June 1944
Time: noon.
Place: 205/217 & 256/268 Amesbury Avenue
A.R.P. Post: K.98

CRICKLADE AVENUE

Two high explosive bombs and an incendiary landed here on 17th October 1940.

AMESBURY AVENUE

Before mid-day the top part of Amesbury Avenue was hit. Police, N.F.S., Heavy and Light Rescue parties, ambulances and doctors were quickly on the scene. There were few K.98 wardens available at that time of day, but willing reinforcements rushed in from surrounding posts. Actually the first Incident Officer was from K.97: Warden Ward - and he carried on until S.W.Sudell of K.98 arrived. D.P.W.Barker returned hurriedly from business and exercised general supervision.

P.W. Charles Gorringe of K.96 took charge at the K.98 post; whilst others present were the Senior District Warden, D.D.W. T.J.Bryant, Canon Salmon, Rector of St.Leonard's Church and head of the Welfare Organisation, and D.W.W.Faulkner of "J" District, who functioned for Mr Belham until P.W.W.Hunt took over.

P.W. John Sumner had received a nasty eye injury from glass, but insisted on remaining at the incident until ordered to hospital by Mr Bryant. It was weeks before he could return to duty, unfortunately minus an eye.

Thanks to the smart work of the parties, plus the accuracy of the occupants' check carried out by Wardens Bayliff and Riches, the operation quickly resolved itself into a search for the family of a Dutchman at number 260 Amesbury Avenue. Mary Linders and the "three lovely children" - as the neighbours described them - aged 2, 3 and 4, were beyond human aid when found.

HITHERFIELD ROAD

A H.E. bomb fell on 56 Hitherfield Road on 15th September 1940.

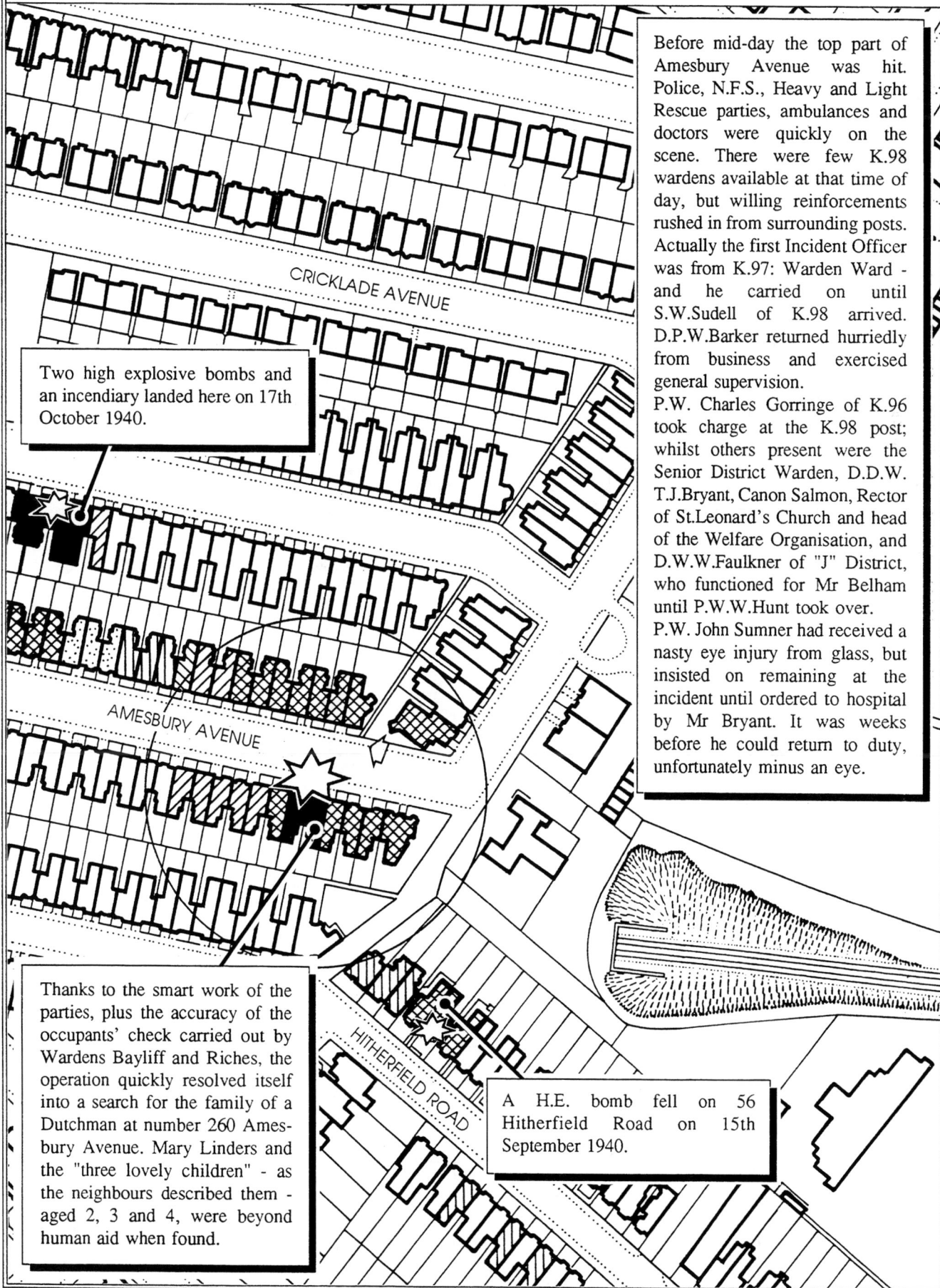

This map is based on the Ordnance Survey 60" map published in 1936

49

Bomb 13

Date: 29th June 1944
Time: 7 p.m.
Place: Sherwood Avenue/Glenister Park Road
A.R.P. Post: J.83

The third flying bomb in 12 hours crashed in the Vale at the apex of Sherwood Avenue and Glenister Park Road, almost on top of Post J.83.

P.W. Fred Joslin immediately took charge as I.O. The turn-out of services was particularly brisk, the N.F.S. being present in very large numbers, also the Home Guard, and both assisted with the rescue work. The Home Guard flung out such an effective cordon that even Mr Bryant couldn't get his car through!

Although damage was considerable, serious casualties were few, but three wardens were injured. Dr Sinclair was again prominent, doing good work.

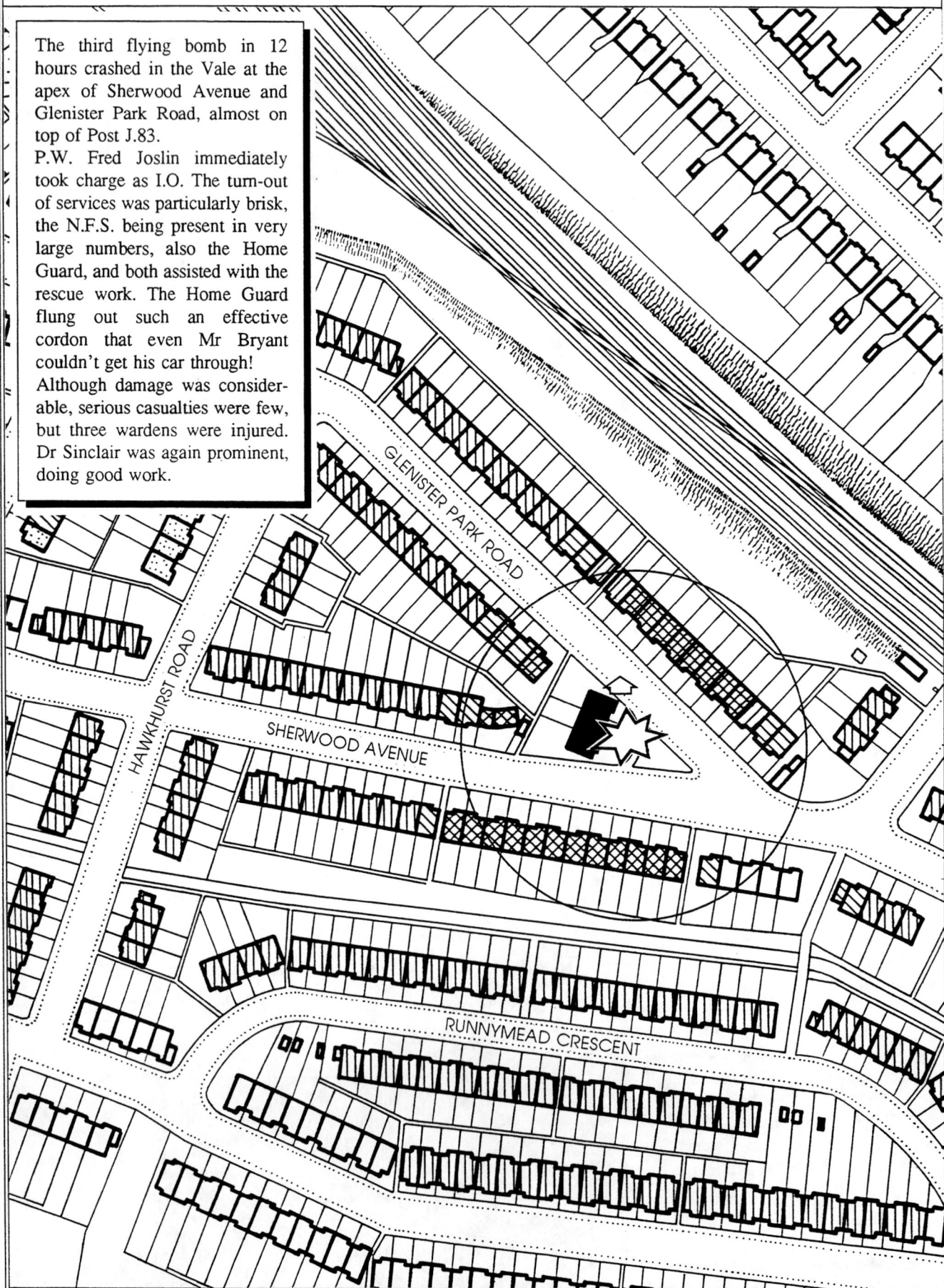

GLENISTER PARK ROAD

HAWKHURST ROAD

SHERWOOD AVENUE

RUNNYMEAD CRESCENT

This map is based on the Ordnance Survey 60" maps published in 1935 and 1936

Bomb 13

Date: 29th June 1944
Time: 7 p.m.
Place: Sherwood Avenue/Glenister Park Road
A.R.P. Post: J.83

Rescuers of many services at Glenister Park Road

Under the guidance of a doctor, a male casualty is lifted onto a stretcher. The Anderson Shelter was in a ground floor room, but the room and house vanished.

Bomb 14

Date: 30th June 1944
Time: 10.30 a.m.
Place: 11 Hoadly Road
A.R.P. Post: K.95

The flying bomb landed mid-morning in Hoadly Road.

One of the homes damaged was that of the Pitts family at number 6. Mrs Nora Pitts was well-known locally as Staff Commandant of the British Red Cross Society and Honorary Secretary of the Penny-a-week Fund. They took their misfortune with typical pluck and humour.

At 9 Hoadly Road lived D.W.W. Eustace Belham. His home was wrecked but none of his family was injured.

The flying bomb landed on 11 Hoadly Road killing an Old English Sheepdog and fatally injuring Miss McSweeney.

D.P.W. Waight was fortunately available to act as I.O., and P.W. Hawes returned from business before operations had been proceeding very long. From the casualty angle this was the "cheapest" fly bomb incident to date, only one person requiring removal to hospital. It was cleared quickly and well.

Mrs Muriel Nutting, Borough Organiser of the W.V.S., immediately offered a room in her house at number 39 for use as the Incident Inquiry Point.

DREWSTEAD ROAD

HOADLY ROAD

This map is based on the Ordnance Survey 60" map published in 1936

Bomb 14

Date: 30th June 1944
Time: 10.30 a.m.
Place: 11 Hoadly Road
A.R.P. Post: K.95

A reminiscence from
Sheila Edwards

I was in the W.R.N.S. in Scotland when Hoadly Road had its flying bomb, which demolished the house opposite us (we were in number 10), killing the old sheep dog, and injuring Miss McSweeney, who was alone in the house. She spent a long time in St.Peter's Hospital, Chertsey, where I visited her when on embarkation leave but I am afraid that she never recovered and died later.

The bomb, as so often happened with blast, completely demolished the McSweeney's house, and the ones on each side had to be demolished, and the two next were seriously damaged, but our house, directly opposite, lost windows and doors, but had no structural damage, nor did the houses on either side.

The search for a trapped casualty goes forward.

"She's alive": The trapped casualty has been reached and is given a drink through rubber tubing.
Meanwhile the Heavy Rescue man in the foreground studies the problem of her release.

Bomb 15

Date: 1st July 1944
Time: afternoon
Place: 34/36 Freshwater Road
A.R.P. Post: I.79

Bomb 15 crashed early in the afternoon on the Wandsworth Borough 1920's housing estate in Freshwater Road. D.D.W. Walter Ames was the Incident Officer, with Mrs B.K.Smith as clerk. D.W.Waight was also prominent, whilst rescue work went forward well under Deputy Station Officer G.Regan. One of the human chains man-handling skips of debris was composed of members of all the Civil Defence services, plus representatives of the Army, R.A.F., Home Guard and civilian passers-by on their way home from work. It was typical of the universal desire to help, a grand spirit which did much to lighten the burden of this period.

St. Paul's Church was badly damaged and unusable. Rev. E.F.L. Henson, who had had the living for 10 years, relinquished it after the incident. The church was re-opened on 7th June 1946.
By a quirk of fate, Rev. Ralph Whitrow, who left St. Paul's in 1934 for Hampshire, was killed on a visit to Westminster about this same time by a flying bomb.

Eight bombs fell in Post I.79 on the night of 30th September 1940. One fell on 165 Welham Road.

Hilda Carter and her young son died when a bomb fell on 86 Salterford Road on 30th September 1940.

Mary Evans of 36 and Wallace Collard of 34 Freshwater Road were killed.

Services arrived quickly and in force, especially the N.F.S. The London Auxiliary Ambulance Service practice which had recently been introduced, of attaching an ambulance to the tail of the convoy of the fire appliances, meant that it was on the scene early. Some casualties were removed in other vehicles and this caused difficulty later, since no record of the names was kept. It meant sending messengers to all likely hospitals to secure lists of admittances, for no incident was ever closed until every person had been accounted for beyond any shadow of doubt.

Mr David Robertson, M.P. for Streatham, arrived at the incident five minutes after it happened, with the Senior District Warden and Divisional Fire Guard, but left immediately, saying it was no place for sightseers, who would merely hamper the services.

WELHAM ROAD

FRESHWATER ROAD

This map is based on the Ordnance Survey 60" maps published in 1933 and 1936

54

Bomb 16

Date: 1st July 1944
Time: afternoon
Place: 47 Rectory Lane
A.R.P. Post: I.79

Just as the situation was becoming clear at the Freshwater Road incident, another bomb landed only 150 yards away in Rectory Lane. All personnel went flat, whilst the mobile canteen with staff inside bounced on its tyres. This was the only occasion that a Streatham post area had two fly bomb incidents in one day, and possibly fired by the same German crew.

The wardens are to be congratulated on the way they just moved over and carried on, with dinner even more remote.

Mr T.Waight, the District Warden, and others ran to the scene and set up the Incident Officer's control point before the cloud of smoke and dust from the explosion had settled. Services came quickly and worked with an efficiency increasing with practice. A slight fire was soon extinguished by the N.F.S.

Five wards of St. Benedict's Hospital were badly blasted, but the First Aid Post under Dr Abrahams was able to function despite a severe shake-up. Later in the incident, Divisional Officer Baker sent N.F.S. working parties to the hospital to clear up and repair the black-out, a much appreciated action.

St.Benedict's Hospital

F.A.P.8

RECTORY LANE

Gertrude Simmons was killed at 50 Rectory Lane.

The total casualties at these two incidents were 66, of which five were fatal, including a passing cyclist in Rectory Lane whose identification was a problem.

CROWBOROUGH ROAD

WELHAM ROAD

Bomb 15 had landed here an hour or so earlier.

IDLECOMBE ROAD

One pathetic sight was to see the efforts being made to salvage the scattered stock of a small shop, whose proprietress was a casualty worrying over her loss.

Alderman Jordan, Deputy Chief Warden, who was present most of the time, expressed himself well-satisfied, and indeed I.79, assisted by wardens from every other post in "I" District, came through this double ordeal very well.

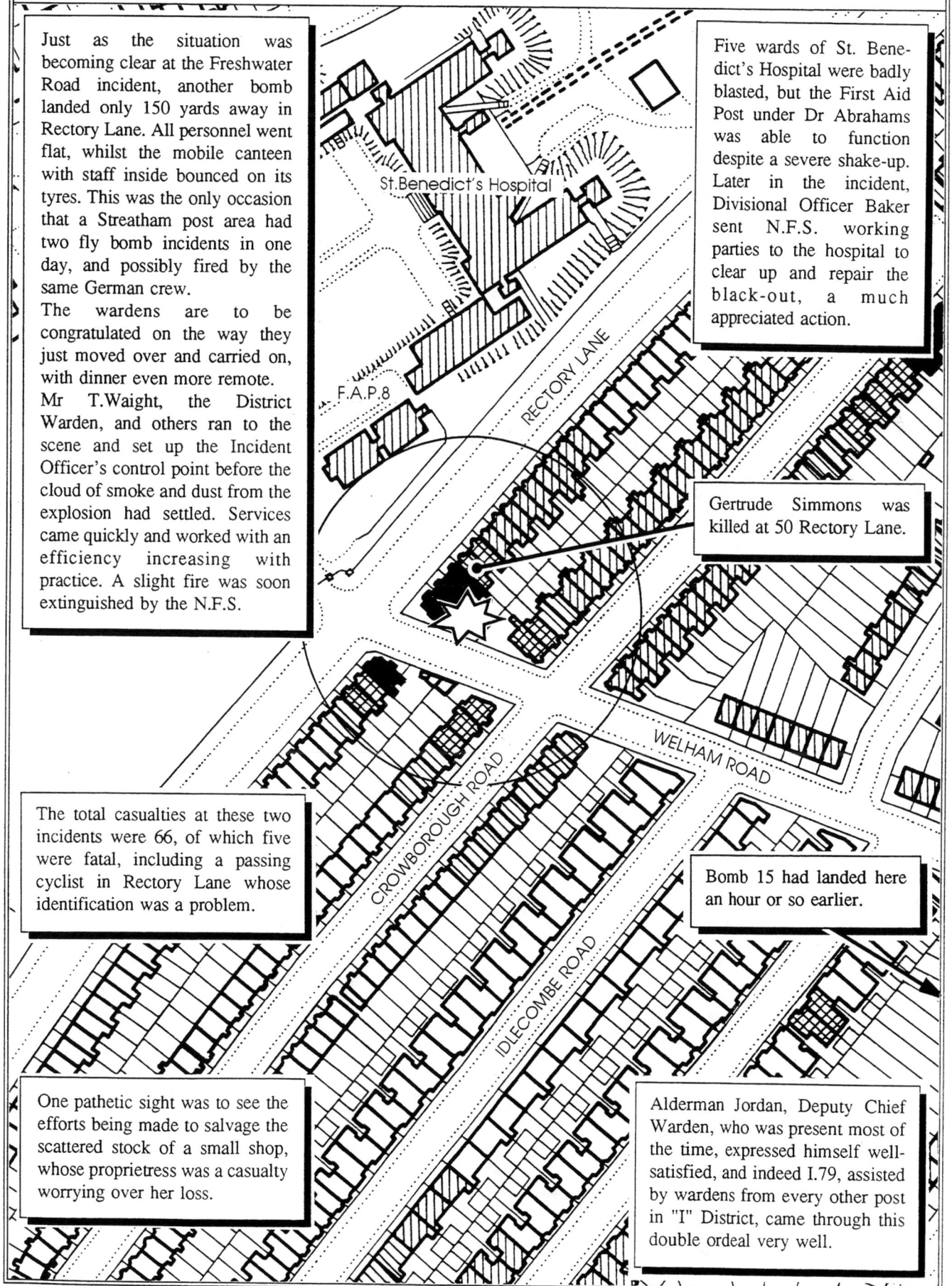

This map is based on the Ordnance Survey 60" map published in 1938

The A.R.P. in Action

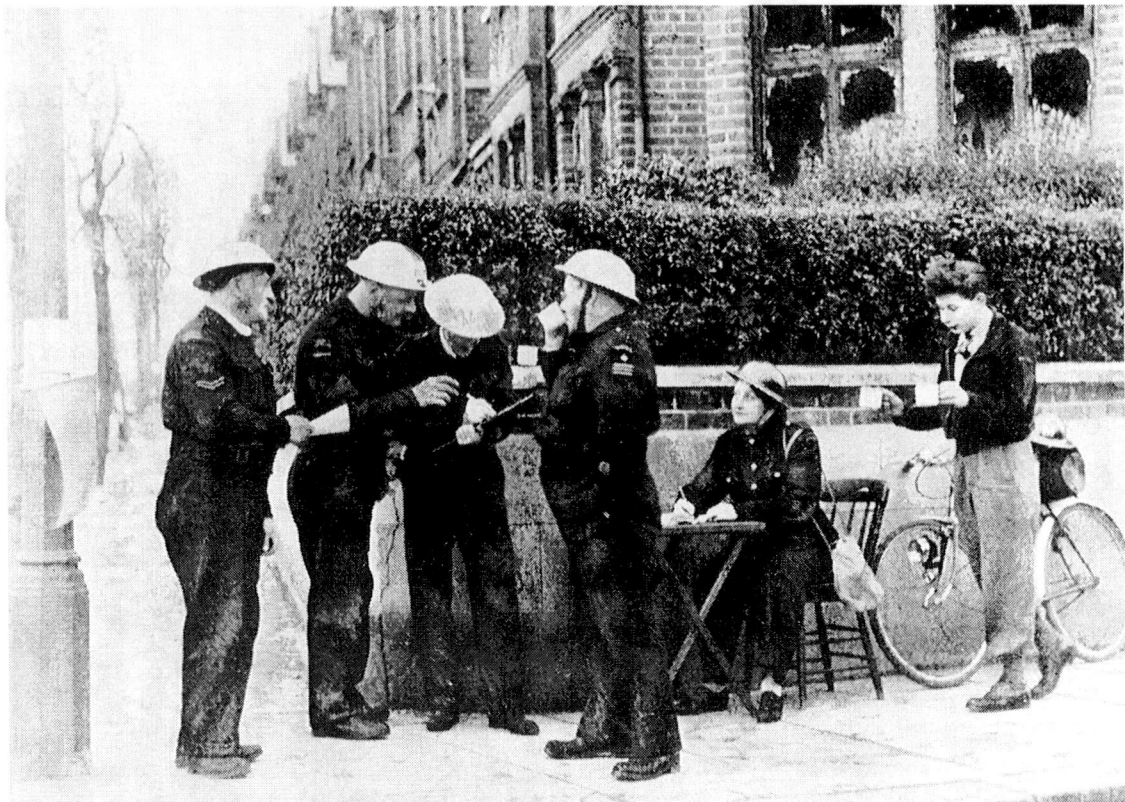

At the Incident Post: The I.O. checks through the list of persons still missing with the L.C.C. Heavy Rescue Officer. Meanwhile, the Senior District Warden takes tea and the C.D. Messenger returns from an important mission. [Bomb 16 - although admitted later to be a posed photograph.]

"The Navy's Here!": The mobile canteen serves tea to naval ratings helping with first aid repairs to properties in the Pendle Road area. W.V.S. from nearby Incident Inquiry Point are also refreshed. [Bomb 35]

Bomb 17

Date: 1st July 1944
Time: p.m.
Place: 19 Aldrington Road
A.R.P. Post: I.81

"I" District received its third flying bomb that day, at Aldrington Road. Fred Archer, only recently appointed Post Warden of I.81, proved an able I.O. and was well supported by the other wardens.

The most severely damaged house was 17 Aldrington Road, the home of Mrs Cronk, a prominent member of the W.V.S. Staying with her for the night was Mrs J.Crisp, the Streatham W.V.S. Sub-Centre Organiser. Her home was in Wimbledon and she had stopped in Streatham from a sheer sense of duty.

Mrs Crisp had taken over the Centre in March 1943 and had endeared herself to everyone with her unfailing kindness, charm and keen sense of humour.

Both she and Mrs Cronk were seriously injured. Mrs Crisp said that although trapped and injured, she was fully conscious and did not doubt for a moment that the Civil Defence services would find and rescue her. Her injuries prevented Mrs Crisp from making another public appearance until May 1945. In her absence, Mrs Knight and Mrs Larlham took up the reins of the Centre.

ALDRINGTON ROAD

St.Alban's Church

St. Alban's Church and hall were partially damaged but services continued.

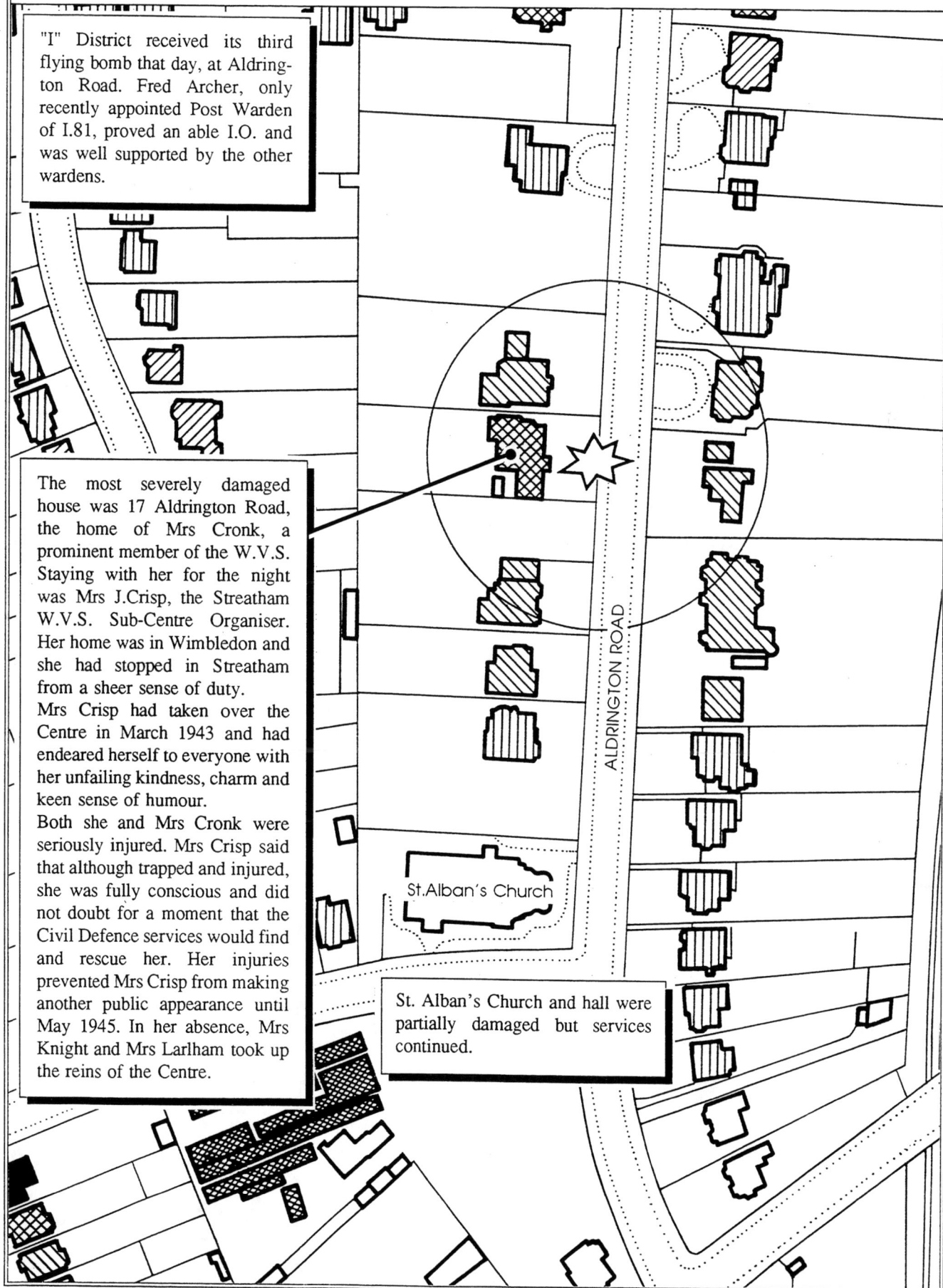

This map is based on the Ordnance Survey 60" map published in 1938

Bomb 18

Date: 3rd July 1944
Time: 5 a.m.
Place: 40 Besley Street
A.R.P. Post: I.78

Just before 5 a.m. a fly bomb crashed on the railway embankment immediately behind a row of houses in Besley Street. Prompt steps were taken by the wardens to advise the railway company in case the track had been rendered unsafe.

Warden Usher of Post I.78 assumed the role of Incident Officer, and a Home Guard Officer reported within a matter of minutes of the bomb falling, despite the early hour. Reinforcements of wardens came from many posts, including J.84, a pleasing instance of inter-district co-operation. Two of the lads who acted as C.D. Messengers (Randall and Letchford) were quickly on the scene from Post I.77.

Parked up among the Fire appliances, thus indicating a very early arrival, was the little green van used by "J" Head Fire Guard S.A.Cotton. There can have been few Streatham incidents at which he was not present, ever-willing to lend a hand at anything, from sweeping roads clear of debris upwards.

In addition to the usual services, the Metropolitan Water Board and Gas Repair Party were also present. Although not spectacular, the work done by these and other Utility Companies was essential to the handling of many incidents.

Number 36 Besley Street had been the home of the Elliott family for 30 years. Mr and Mrs Frank Elliott with a son and daughter were in the Anderson shelter when the V-1 demolished their house. Fragments of the bomb penetrated the shelter killing Mr Elliott and severely injuring the others. The survivors were sent to hospital and the women were under treatment for five months, inflicted with terrible scars. Every scrap of furniture was lost, but Mrs Elliott remained cheerful, saying she was lucky to be alive.

Three members of the Wood family living at number 40 were killed, including Charles Wood, a Fire Guard.

Pamela Freeborn was living at 8 Edgington Road at the time, and tells her story opposite.

Many of these small terrace houses were occupied by elderly folk, and the spirit they displayed was splendid. Well could the I.O. reply to the routine question "Morale? Excellent."

There were 27 casualties at this incident, four of which were fatal. The rescue operations were completed in three hours, and permission to close the incident was granted by the Controller at 8 a.m.

This map is based on the Ordnance Survey 60" map published in 1936

Bomb 18

Date: 3rd July 1944
Time: 5 a.m.
Place: 40 Besley Street
A.R.P. Post: I.78

A day or so later, the local M.P. (Mr David Robertson) was visiting the scene, and called at one of the blitzed houses. The husband asked him in and through to the kitchen, where mother was sitting with her legs in a bath of hot water "to get the swelling down a bit." She was full of praise for father, who had spent the day cleaning the debris from the loft, without any outside help. Then jointly they drew attention to the grandfather clock, which nearly reached the ceiling, the case of which was studded with fragments of glass which the explosion had driven in. "But it never stopped, sir, not for minute," they exclaimed with pride.

"Why don't you go to the Rest Centre for a spell?" they were asked. "Well, we did try it, and everyone was most kind - but we are both over seventy and would rather be here in our own home." "How do you manage for cooking?" "Ah, that is a bit trying, for the gas-stove is in the outhouse, with no roof, windows or door left, and often when I go back the gas has blown out." "Have you any family who could help you clear up?" "Well, we have some sons and daughters, but they are all married with homes of their own and we haven't told them that we've been bombed, for they would only worry about us, and we can manage all right, thank you."

An account of Bomb 18 from across the tracks
by Pamela Davis (née Freeborn)

The Doodlebug which I recall most vividly fell on Besley Street in the early hours of 4th July 1944 - my fifteenth birthday! I lived in an upstairs maisonette at 8 Edgington Road which was separated from Besley Street by the railway line and received the full force of the blast.

We had been sleeping in the street air-raid shelter and I was woken by someone lifting part of the shelter door off my bunk. There was a cloud of dust everywhere as we all went outside and it was impossible to see anything clearly for a few minutes. At last we were able to assess the damage and my father managed to climb the stairs to see whether it was safe enough inside for my mother and myself to enter. We had no roof, no ceilings, no windows and no front door on our home. There was plaster and rubble everywhere. Our cat, who always took shelter under a tin bath during raids, emerged with a bump on his head and covered in dust. Our canary was killed by falling plaster but, fortunately, they were the only casualties in our road.

I suddenly remembered the dress which my mother had made from a remnant for a birthday present - it was still hanging in the wardrobe but had been torn to shreds by flying glass. The birthday cake, made by carefully saving rations, had disappeared, so had a rice pudding and a vase of Sweet Williams. All of these had been blasted through the window and were never seen again. It took me more than 40 years before I could bring myself to have Sweet Williams indoors again.

We heard footsteps on the stairs - it was the postman with my birthday cards. He said, "There's no door to post anything through, so I've brought these upstairs."

By then it was pouring with rain. The dust turned to mud and everything we still possessed got soaked. We had no gas supply but someone from Eardley Road came along with some tea and a sandwich.

Later that day my form mistress from the school I attended -

Streatham Hill & Clapham High School - arrived to say that the school had also been badly damaged and was being evacuated to Halifax in a day or so and would I go with them. I declined - having spent the whole of the war in Streatham I had no intention of leaving then.

Eventually some tarpaulins arrived and they kept the rain out. My birthday tea consisted of bread and jam eaten sitting on the doorstep with a friend! It was a birthday I shall never forget as long as I live!

I cannot say what the casualties were in Besley Street - I believe there were some - but I do know that one elderly gentleman was in bed when the doodlebug exploded. His house was demolished but he was found unhurt - still in bed - unable to move as the bed was swaying above a sheer drop where he had to stay until rescued.

Bomb 19

Date: 3rd July 1944
Time: 7 a.m.
Place: Streatham Hill Theatre
A.R.P. Post: K.97

Whilst rescue operations were still proceeding at Besley Street, another bomb was seen to fall on Streatham Hill. Senior officers hurried to the new incident in their cars. Warden Ward acted as Incident Officer.

An electricty sub-station was damaged and residents were without power for some days after the explosion.

F.Penny lived at 26 Killieser Avenue. His story is opposite.

The theatre management had permitted members of the staff and their friends to sleep in the underground bars and lounges as a kind of de-luxe shelter. Immediately the N.F.S. and Rescue parties penetrated into this part of the theatre and conducted a thorough search. Some casualties were quickly recovered and despatched to hospital, including Thomas Bryant, the "K" Deputy District Warden, also his wife and son, who were sheltering there since their own home had been wrecked in an earlier incident. Later, Mrs Bryant's mother, Mrs Emma Jones was recovered, but unfortunately she was dead. Mr Bryant made a good recovery but he was advised to take a prolonged convalescence in the Isle of Wight.

Barrhill Road was covered with the displaced brickwork, making it impassible for vehicles.

The Streatham Hill Theatre received a blast to its side, blowing an enormous hole in the wall and demolishing some of the circle balcony. Built as a number one touring theatre in 1929, it had modified its programmes to twice-nightly variety during the war. The bomb on Wyatt Park Mansions a fortnight earlier had damaged the theatre and it had ceased its operations temporarily.

The Gaumont Palace Cinema, although several yards away was also blast damaged sufficiently for it to close operations for several years.

Special praise is due to Senior Fire Guard Eggleton for the way he carried out his duties, notwithstanding the fact that his wife had been taken to hospital seriously injured.

BLAIRDERRY ROAD

STREATHAM HILL

BARRHILL ROAD

This map is based on the Ordnance Survey 60" map published in 1936

Bomb 19

Date: 3rd July 1944
Time: 7 a.m.
Place: Streatham Hill Theatre
A.R.P. Post: K.97

A reminiscence from
Christine MacLennen

My father, Edward MacLennen, was going to work as a Police Inspector at the Borough Police Station, Southwark. The time would be somewhere between 4.30 - 5.00 a.m. When he heard the V-1 plus the tram coming, the tram driver slowed down for him to catch it, which he did otherwise he would have been at the tram stop near the Theatre and either killed or badly injured. When the tram got to Telford Avenue, it stopped and everybody dived off to take any cover they could find. After the V-1 dropped, they got on the tram again and carried on their journey to work. Dad ran for that tram. He was not a person who would do that unless it was the last resort!

We were in shelters under the shops between Barcombe and Cricklade Avenues. I heard the bang and rumble of the bricks coming down. Also at the same time, two American soldiers fell into the shelter from the main road entrance.

A reminiscence from
F. Penny

I lived at 26 Killieser Avenue. The V-1 fell on the Theatre and woke us up with the rear of the house badly damaged. The blast took the rear roof off, the windows and all the ceilings. We had no electricity as the substation was at the back of the Theatre. All you could see of the old Theatre was a twisted jungle of iron girders which supported the roof.

We had to clear the plaster off the stairs before we could go up, and it took us several days to clear the plaster into the streets. We were lucky that the slates on the roof were put back in about two days and we were able to live in the house. Emergency repairers also replaced the ceilings with plaster board and wood battens across the joins. At the rear of our back garden was a 6ft brick wall which was blown down but that was not replaced until after the war.

For the first two days, having no electricity or gas, we got our meals at the cafe in Sternhold Avenue by the Station.

The side of the Theatre showing damage to the auditorium and stage area

Bomb 20

Date: 3rd July 1944
Time:
Place: Buckleigh Road
A.R.P. Post: J.86

The third bomb that day fell in Buckleigh Road, and extensive damage was done there, and also in Northanger and other adjoining roads. Q.R.C.D.Letts, who worked nearby, and like many other part-time wardens was wearing his uniform ready for such emergencies, dashed round on his cycle, first to the incident, then to Post J.87 to get the warden on duty to send in the Express Report. Returning in quick time, he just beat the first two N.F.S. teams, who immediately searched the damaged properties, recovered many of the casualties and despatched them to hospital. Wardens from J.86 had by then arrived and set up an incident control, D.P.W.Osborn being in charge. Some very good first aid was carried out by the wardens on this occasion.

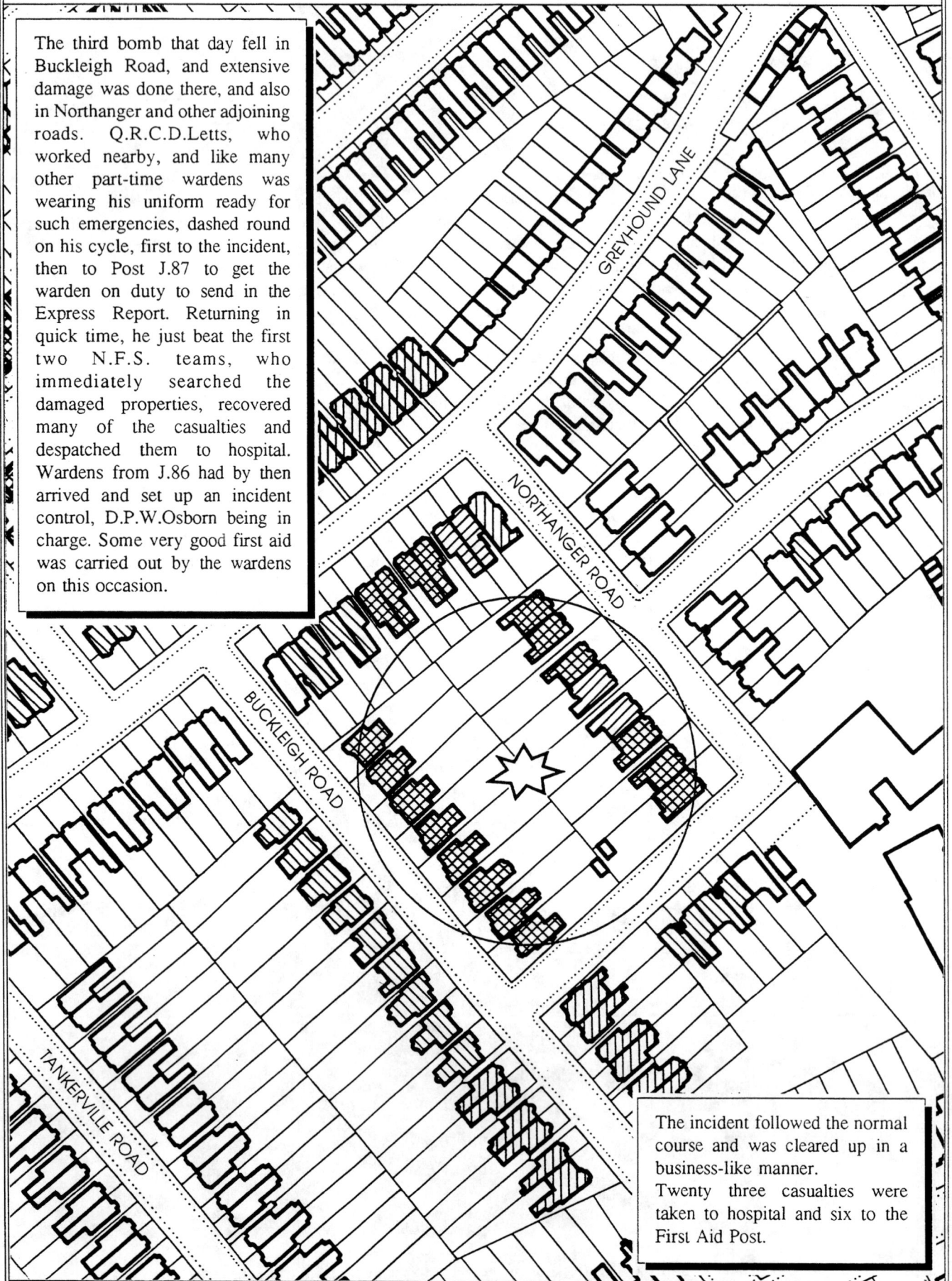

GREYHOUND LANE

NORTHANGER ROAD

BUCKLEIGH ROAD

TANKERVILLE ROAD

The incident followed the normal course and was cleared up in a business-like manner.
Twenty three casualties were taken to hospital and six to the First Aid Post.

This map is based on the Ordnance Survey 60" map published in 1936

Bomb 21

Date: 3rd July 1944
Time: 6.30 p.m.
Place: 93 Kingsmead Road
A.R.P. Post: K.100

This was to prove Streatham's busiest day with the fourth bomb in the space of 14 hours falling on Kingsmead Road.
D.W.P. Harold Grose arrived early and took charge, finding the N.F.S. already well down to the job of reconnaissance.

St.Simon and St.Jude's Church and the adjoining hall were damaged, a short time before members of a youth club were due to meet there.

Among the homeless was P.W. Robert Fraser of 93 Kingsmead. Unable to get rehoused locally, he continued to carry out his duties as part-time warden in Streatham and he was only one of many similarly placed, who showed the same spirit of loyalty, often travelling long and awkward journeys to perform their spells of duty, when it would have been so easy to apply for a transfer to a new and quieter district.

Owing to the lay-out of the streets, control of this K.100 incident could have been very awkward, but K.98, under D.P.W.Barker, immediately took over the damage in the Hillside Road Area, and kept I.O.Grose well posted with what was going on there. Dr Margaret Melvin and Dr Janet McGill were present, also Sister Rogers of F.A.P.5; Mrs Perryman, Welfare Warden for K.100, did good work, so did Mr Redpath, a chemist of Norwood Road, and Mrs Skinner of the W.V.S.

From the casualty angle this was a "cheap" incident, there being only three and they were minor. During the attacks the number of casualties formed a yard-stick by which Civil Defence compared incidents, but it does not do to overlook the enormous amount of suffering inflicted on those who were rendered homeless, or left with no windows, no doors, ceilings down and half a roof. And the weather - it rained! and rained!! and rained!!! multiplying the damage and hardship tenfold.

This map is based on the Ordnance Survey 60" map published in 1936

Bomb 22

Date: 5th July 1944
Time: 1 a.m.
Place: 1a/1b Leigham Vale
A.R.P. Post: K.96

The next bomb crashed in the middle of the night on some shops and houses in Leigham Vale, demolishing several and wrecking many more.

Lambeth A.R.P. were called out to attend damage some half a mile from the blast.

The K.96 wardens were at their action station only 80 yards from the bomb, and in consequence were all injured, or at least, severely shaken.
K.92 stepped into the breach excellently and S.W.Morley, of this post, acted as I.O., assisted by others until D.P.W. Halstead Groves of K.96 arrived and took over, carrying on without a break for ten hours and discharging the responsibility very well.

A father and his son were killed at 1d Leigham Vale (see full story opposite).

ROMEYN ROAD

LEIGHAM VALE

LEIGHAM COURT ROAD

Warden Underwood sustained a head injury, which subsequently necessitated four stitches, but nevertheless, he ran a quarter of a mile to his post, where P.W. Charles Gorringe was on duty. Before entering he had the presence of mind to call out, "Don't be alarmed but I'm bleeding a bit." After delivering his report, he was bandaged and laid on the floor until an ambulance could take him to hospital.

Most of the casualties were recovered quickly and despatched to hospital or the First Aid Post.

This map is based on the Ordnance Survey 60" map published in 1935

Bomb 22

Date: 5th July 1944
Time: 1 a.m.
Place: 1a/1b Leigham Vale
A.R.P. Post: K.96

The census cards indicated there was a family of four sheltering in a reinforced room of 1d Leigham Vale which looked just a mound of debris. By the lights of N.F.S. vehicles plus electric hand lamps, the Rescue Parties under Station Officer Pavey set to work on this task. It proved a long and stubborn rescue, the rubble was so small that it had to be hand-picked away to avoid collapse on the trapped victims below. At last contact was made.

The father, Francis Russell, and his son, John, aged 7, were dead. Another hour or two passed before the hole could be enlarged sufficiently to bring out the first casualty, daughter Jane, aged four. A Dr Russell had been standing by all the time and under his guidance the mother and the girl had been given liquid through a rubber tube. Carefully the Light Rescue men carried the stretcher to a waiting ambulance. There, with the aid of a nurse, the doctor carried out a rapid examination, all the time chatting away to the child giving reassuring answers to her questions about her brother "who went to school." Miraculously it seemed that she was almost unmarked and after another drink, which she insisted having through the rubber tubing again, she was rushed away to hospital for anti-shock treatment.

Meanwhile, the Rescue men found it impossible to extricate the mother, who was showing a marvellous spirit, until the other child was removed from her side. She did not know he was dead, and the men lied with infinite understanding and sympathy: "We shall have to cover your face with a handkerchief to keep the dirt and plaster off while we shift this piece of wood." Again the careful journey to the ambulance for the doctor's examination and for a few moments hope leapt up as rumour flew round the incident that the boy was alive, but alas it was without foundation.

From the heap of debris on the left two live casualties were recovered and two dead.
One of the wrecked shops was the wardens' action station.

Bomb 23

Date: 5th July 1944
Time: about 2 p.m.
Place: War Memorial, Streatham Common
A.R.P. Post: J.89

Winesses saw the fly bomb making its descent towards open ground when it appeared to change its course suddenly, crashed into a tree in the War Memorial Garden, then landed on the pavement below, wrecking a police box and the wardens' post, also numerous shops in the High Road. The blast tore down the tree, scattering leaves everywhere. The Senior District Warden arrived on the scene with Q.R.C.D.Letts and decided to act as I.O. himself as Post J.89 was out of action, Warden Webb being severely injured and his wife, also a warden, was a casualty too.

First Aid Post No.6 at Streatham Baths had a busy afternoon, nearly 50 casualties being dealt with from this incident. The only fatality was Arthur Searle at a Chinese Club.

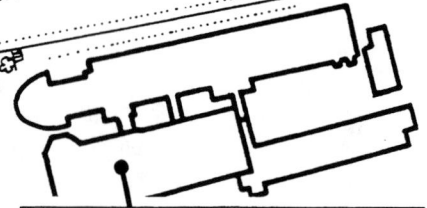

Coventry Hall, the depot of Heavy Rescue, was damaged but a party from there turned out promptly.

The Congregational Church was damaged and services had to be held in the crypt.

By a miracle there were no buses or trams passing at the time, but the driver of an approaching tram had the presence of mind to brake hard as he saw the bomb dive and shouted to his passengers to duck, which they all did, thus avoiding injury.

Mr Ivor Jones, 396 High Road, was in the back of his chemist shop but escaped unhurt. He immediately gave useful information on other shopkeepers and residents.

The War Memorial, erected to the memory of those killed during the 1914-18 War, was undamaged.

Fortunately, being early closing day, the only customers were in the hairdressers. The owner, Marion, her son, mother, two assistants and two customers just had time to dive into the safest spot available. A soldier, knowing his wife was at the saloon, rushed to the scene and helped the N.F.S and C.D. units dig out the survivors suffering from shock, bruises and cuts.

After the last ambulance had been dismissed it was reported that yet another casualty had been discovered in a wrecked licensed club. Upon further investigation, however, by no less a person than the Borough Controller himself, it was reported that the casualty's condition was the result of opportunist stocktaking prior to abandoning the premises, rather than direct enemy action.

The police were requested to make a temporary traffic diversion, which they did, but in less than a quarter of an hour it was possible to dispense with this. Whilst the inevitable dislocation was at its height a military convoy went past and a lorry full of Americans pulled up and offered help. Knowing that control was in train and adequate C.D. services present, they were declined with thanks, assuring them that "everything is O.K." They looked round at the scene of devastation, shrugged their shoulders and saying, "Right-O, bud," continued on their way, doubtless musing on the queer ways of the British.

The difficulty of knowing how many people might have been passing and blown into the shops as they collapsed, meant the search had to be thorough and intensive - and it certainly was.

This map is based on the Ordnance Survey 60" maps published in 1935 and 1936

Bomb 23

Date: 5th July 1944
Time: afternoon
Place: War Memorial, Streatham Common
A.R.P. Post: J.89

Streatham High Road taken only a few moments after the bomb fell. The picture shows the orderly search for casualties in the shops and the calm reaction of the public, police and tram staff. These shops were never rebuilt and the space exists as Streatham's last remaining bomb site.

A casualty is helped along to the nearby First Aid Post at the Swimming Baths.

Bomb 24

Date: 6th July 1944
Time: 8 a.m.
Place: 37 Southcroft Road
A.R.P. Post: I.79

The bomb crashed in Southcroft Road at the junction of Salterford Road and made an unusually wide and deep crater. This was to prove a fairly long and difficult incident, there being 46 casualties, including three fatal. Two other persons died later in hospital. P.W. Fred Greetham endeavoured to 'phone through the Express Report a minute after the explosion but there was a hold-up, and a cyclist messenger had to be despatched. Mr Waight, the "I" D.W. took charge as I.O., with Miss Windridge as clerk, and both had a narrow escape when part of a damaged house collapsed around them. D.P.W.Smith took over as I.O. in the later stages.

An extremely deaf lady had a marvellous escape, for she must have been within 15 feet of the bomb when it exploded. Later in the day, after treatment for head and wrist injuries, she was to be seen carrying tea to the rescue parties.

Winifred Troke of 39 Southcroft Road died in the blast.

Elderly Alice Barton and her daughter, Dora, of number 41 Southcroft Road, died later in St.James's Hospital.

SOUTHCROFT ROAD

The tram-track was quickly cleared and the L.P.T.B. crane which arrived was not needed. Passengers on passing trams had a grand-stand view of the rescue operations.

Grandfather Daniel Hall of 96 Southcroft Road died next day from his injuries.

The services included some from Mitcham, while wardens from Post G.59 (Tooting) gave welcome help during the day.

The operations of the afternoon became a search for Eric Russell, a thirteen year old, who had been delivering newspapers in South-croft Road when the bomb fell. Commandant Wilson of the Light Rescue Service, knew the boy and gave valuable help, whilst Wardens Grindrod and Mills traced out his calls from house to house and eventually located the exact spot, where search revealed first his bag of papers and then the boy himself, who must have been killed instantly.

Characteristic of the spirit of fun shown by many in acute adversity was the man who ran out of his wrecked home, where he was endeavouring to salvage some of his belongings, crying, "Look what I've found! Look what I've got!" - holding up for all to see - an unbroken egg.

In some of the collapsed houses there was an element of doubt as to the number of persons present when the bomb fell, since it was the time when people would be setting out for work. Several enquiries were made by the police from employers to resolve these queries. In one house the W.A.A.F. daughter was believed to be home, but the first hat to be found contained another name, which led to the discovery that the daughter's friend - also a W.A.A.F. - had stayed there overnight.

This map is based on the Ordnance Survey 60" map published in 1936

Bomb 25

Date: 8th July 1944
Time: late p.m.
Place: 9 Oakdale Road
A.R.P. Post: J.89

In the late evening, L.A.C.Marks was looking out of Divisional Office watching a military convoy move south, when a doodle-bug was heard approaching. It cut out, dived and exploded with a shattering roar and the inevitable cloud of dust and debris shot into the air. Dashing downstairs with the S.D.W., they jumped into a car, hooted their way across the stream of traffic and quickly reached the scene of the incident at the junction of Oakdale and Grasmere Roads. Pulling out the folding table and chair which were always carried in the back of the car, and donning the I.O.'s blue hat cover, the S.D.W. took over just as D.D.W. Edward Tinson, who lived at 16 Valleyfield Road, fought his way through the still thick cloud of dust to exclaim "Hullo, were you sitting there waiting for it?"
Other rescue workers were on the spot in no time, and people who had themselves been blasted out and badly shaken, took up shovels and began to dig for their trapped neighbours.

P. Ormond-Jones, of Post J.91, who had been acting as clerk, relieved Mr Bryant as I.O., and after a spell of seven hours or so, he, in turn, handed over to C. Ford of J.89.
Similarly, Mr Pavey handed over to Mr G.A. Strudwick, and shortly after mid-day of the 9th, the last casualty was recovered.

All three occupants of number 10 Oakdale Road were killed when their home was demolished.

At number 11, after the explosion, Mrs Meldrum emerged from under the stairs into the front room. At that moment, a piano fell through from the floor above and tore off one of her ear-rings as it passed, but left her unscathed. Two wonderful escapes in two minutes.

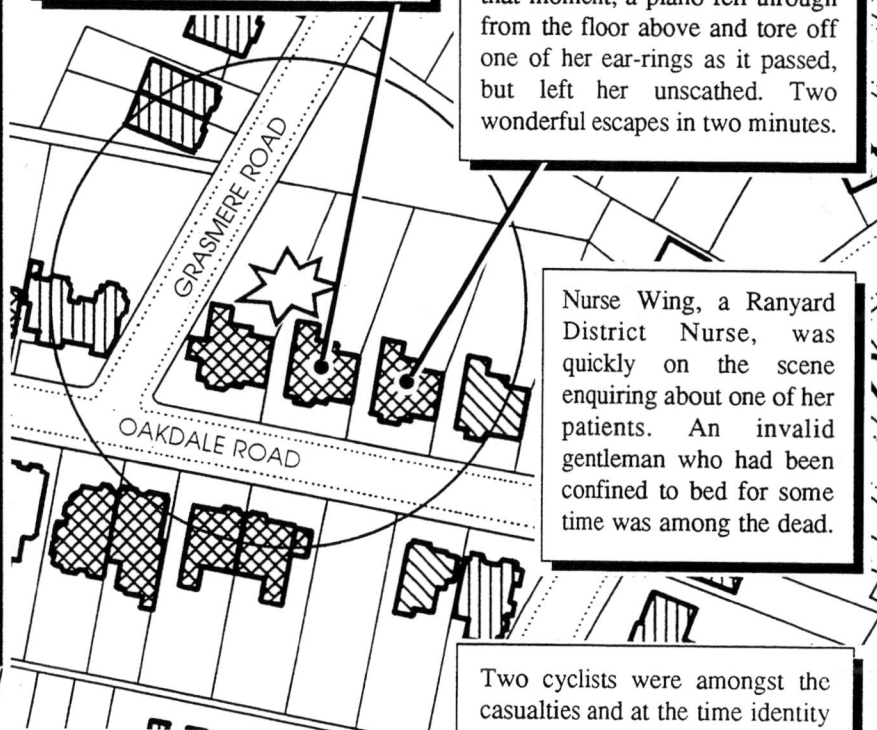

Nurse Wing, a Ranyard District Nurse, was quickly on the scene enquiring about one of her patients. An invalid gentleman who had been confined to bed for some time was among the dead.

Two cyclists were amongst the casualties and at the time identity was difficult to ascertain. Dorothy Dunning, aged 23, was killed outside number 31 Oakdale Road.

All night long the search continued under the efficient leadership of Station Officer D.J.Pavey of the L.C.C. Heavy Rescue Party Service. Persons were missing in four houses and consequently it was necessary to employ a large number of working parties. Commandant A.W.Wilson, in charge of the Streatham Light Rescue parties, was to be seen throughout this long incident, as he was with most of the bombing incidents.

The two sides of Oakdale Road were in different post areas, but the wardens of both J.89 and J.91 rallied to the incident. The damage was extensive and with the houses being large there was a lot of rescue work to be done.

A baby was rescued alive after being buried for several hours. The mother smiled cheerfully to her rescuers as she was lifted to safety in the early hours of the following morning.

Although the occupants' cards stood the test very well, there was a query whether a certain lady who had been away staying with a daughter had returned or not. Before this could be settled, it meant phone calls to the Admiralty and thence to Scotland. Sad to say, the lady had returned that very day and lost her life.

The Rev. Oscar de Berry was about, collecting more bombed-out persons for 'bed and breakfast' at the Immanuel vicarage. At one time he had no less than 19 staying there: Christianity in action.

This map is based on the Ordnance Survey 60" map published in 1938

Bomb 26

Date: 10th July 1944
Time: afternoon
Place: Sherwood Avenue
A.R.P. Post: J.84

The allotments behind Sherwood Avenue received a bomb in the afternoon, not far from an earlier incident, so that for most of the property it was a second dose, but no easier to bear for all that. Casualties were fairly light and none fatal. Being day-time, the wardens came from various posts and D.P.W.Harrison of J.87 acted as I.O.

Post J.84

Several bombs were dropped in the area on the night of 15th October 1940.

A woman and her son, whose house was smashed to bits, were saved from injury by the Anderson shelter to which they had run as the bomb approached. Shortly afterwards, when they were calmly discussing their narrow escape with a press photographer, the mother suddenly broke off and exclaimed with a little cry, "Oh, George, look! our two lovely strawberry plants have gone from the top of the shelter," and it really seemed to distress her more at the moment than the loss of her home.

An earlier V-1 dropped in the culvert on 22nd June.

This map is based on the Ordnance Survey 60" map published in 1936

Bomb 26

Date: 10th July 1944
Time: afternoon
Place: Sherwood Avenue
A.R.P. Post: J.84

"We were in there." A young man and his mother (wearing overall) dashed from the house on the right to the Anderson shelter as the bomb approached and so escaped injury. Pieces of the bomb are in the foreground.

A district nurse directs N.F.S. personnel lowering a woman casualty to a stretcher. The water bottle indicates a member of the Light Rescue Party.

71

Bomb 27

Date: 13th July 1944
Time: evening
Place: Streatham Common
A.R.P. Post: J.86

It was a beautiful summer's evening when Bomb 27 fell on Streatham Common. P.Ormond-Jones, the Post Warden of J.91, acted as Incident Officer.

The services were on the spot in record time and made a brave show, for instead of being spread, as usual, over several streets, they were parked in one long line. No less than 25 N.F.S vehicles reported, and with all the other services there must have been a total of nearly fifty. S.W.Lawman was kept busy controlling the traffic, the bulk of which was quickly returned to depot.

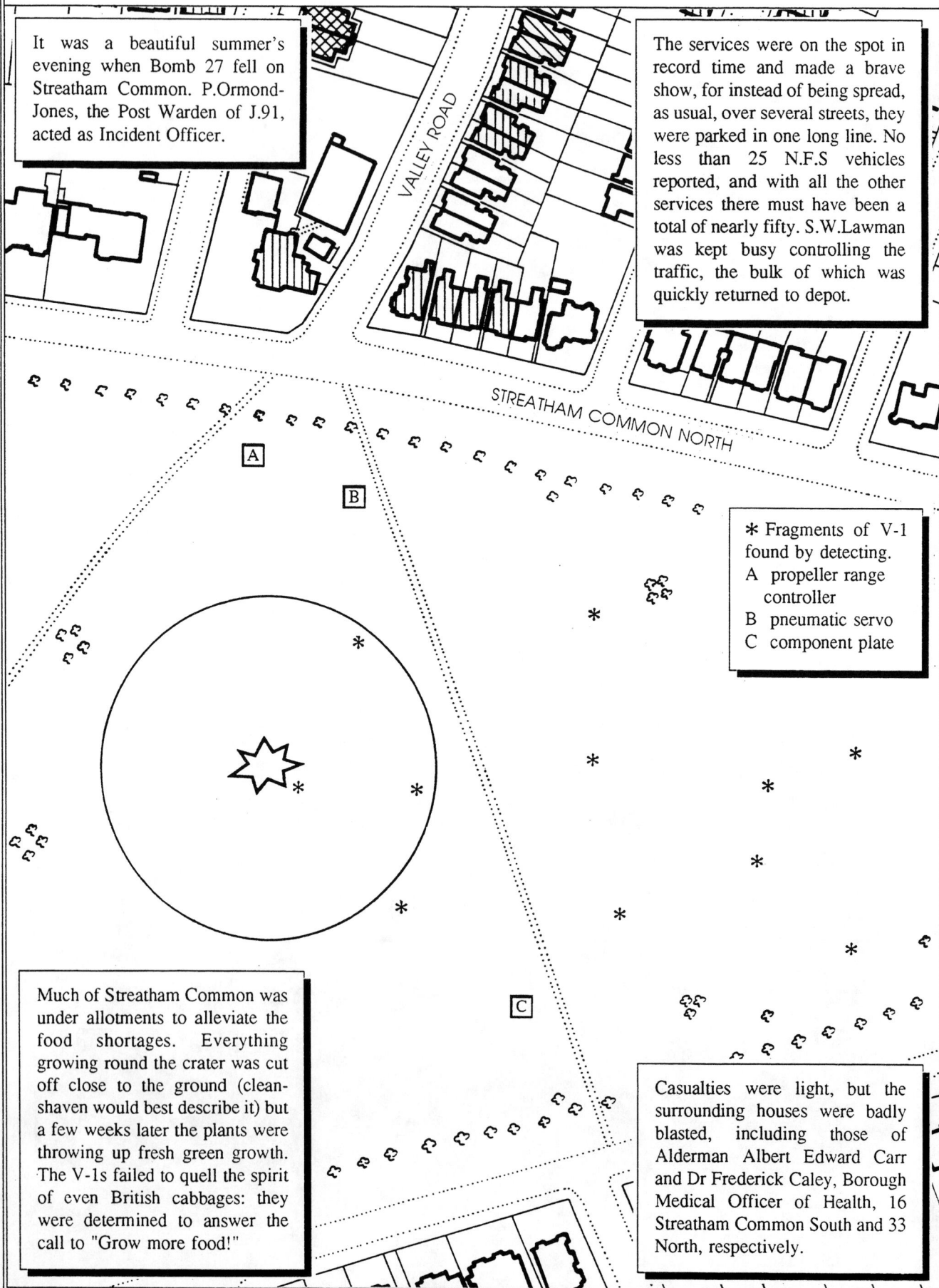

VALLEY ROAD

STREATHAM COMMON NORTH

* Fragments of V-1 found by detecting.
A propeller range controller
B pneumatic servo
C component plate

Much of Streatham Common was under allotments to alleviate the food shortages. Everything growing round the crater was cut off close to the ground (clean-shaven would best describe it) but a few weeks later the plants were throwing up fresh green growth. The V-1s failed to quell the spirit of even British cabbages: they were determined to answer the call to "Grow more food!"

Casualties were light, but the surrounding houses were badly blasted, including those of Alderman Albert Edward Carr and Dr Frederick Caley, Borough Medical Officer of Health, 16 Streatham Common South and 33 North, respectively.

This map is based on the Ordnance Survey 60" map published in 1940

Bomb 28

Date: 18th July 1944
Time:
Place: Covington Way
A.R.P. Post: J.91

Mrs Pamela Osborne recalls:

"I can remember standing on the kitchen doorstep of our house in Covington Way watching the flying bombs come over. As soon as the engine cut out we would run to the Morrison shelter, which we had in the lounge. One landed just into the Rookery, a little further down the road from us. The blast blew out our windows and the back bedroom ceiling fell down and a large hole appeared between the front and back bedrooms. Strangely, the blast blew the back door and the front door in so that they met in the hall! My mother was saved from injury be being in the shelter as the lounge door fell on top of it. The Rev. O.K. de Berry and the Rev. Stephens were soon round meeting on our front step to make sure we were alright. The A.R.P. came to dig people out from the lower 8 houses, some of which were then uninhabitable, being later on rebuilt. The A.R.P. boarded up our window spaces, and the sailors came round to put the tiles back."

A fly bomb landed in part of the Rookery Gardens, setting alight the top of large tree.
D.P.W. Stanley Chaplin of J.85 handled the incident.

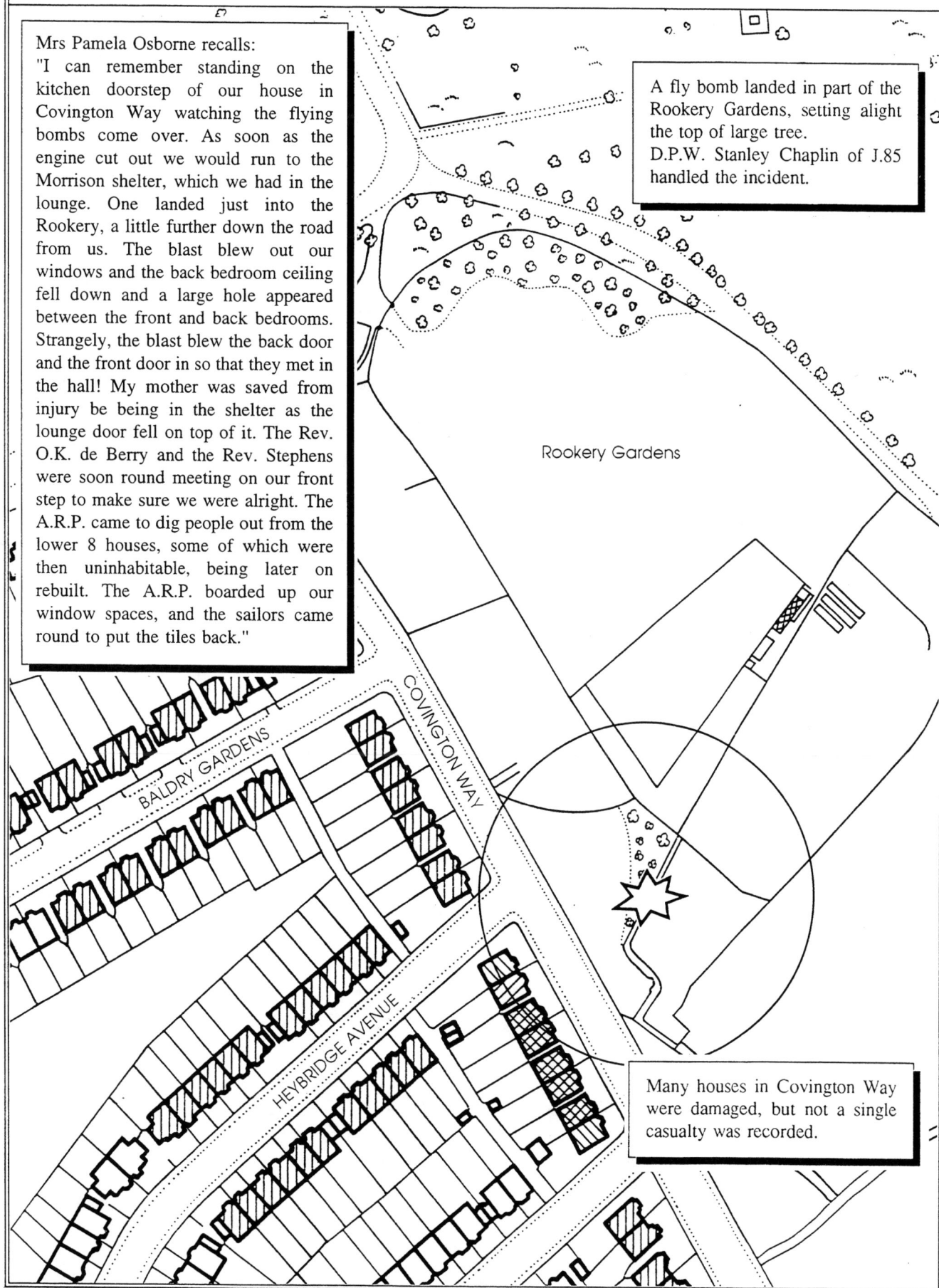

Rookery Gardens

COVINGTON WAY

BALDRY GARDENS

HEYBRIDGE AVENUE

Many houses in Covington Way were damaged, but not a single casualty was recorded.

This map is based on the Ordnance Survey 60" map published in 1936

Bomb 29

Date: 21st July 1944
Time: 5 a.m.
Place: 144 Moyser Road
A.R.P. Post: I.80

The bomb fell just before light at the junction of Moyser Road and Furzedown Drive. The scene of devastation appeared particularly widespread, although as it proved, casualties were not numerous.

D.W. Thomas Waight acted as I.O. and was well served by the personnel of I.80 and the reinforcements from neighbouring posts.

This corner of Streatham received attention from bombers during the historic raids on the capital.

These bombs fell on 29th December 1940 during the infamous fire attack on the capital.

Two bombs fell during the last raid of the Blitz.

FURZEDOWN DRIVE

DALESIDE ROAD

CROWBOROUGH ROAD

During the fourth day of the early raids - on 11th September 1940 - the area received several H.E. bombs and 2 oil bombs.

Warrant Officer Donald Alden and his young wife were killed at 17 Furzedown Drive.

Post I.80

MOYSER ROAD

The N.F.S., Rescue parties, Home Guard and Fire Guards all co-operated in the search for casualties, and rapid progress was made. A bulldozer helped clear the roads of debris.

Admiral Sir Edward Evans, one of London's Regional Commissioners visited the incident, expressed satisfaction at the operations, sampled the Streatham mobile canteen's tea, signed the post log-book, took the address of a crippled ex-service man and left. The latter subsequently received £5 from a fund donated from South Africa, and the Admiral also sent a box of cigarettes to the wardens - a much appreciated gesture.

The W.V.S. under Mrs Irwin, the District Leader, did very good work and opened up the Inquiry Point in the wardens' stand-by post, operating for some time.

This map is based on the Ordnance Survey 60" maps published in 1936 and 1937

Bomb 29

Date: 21st July 1944
Time: 5 a.m.
Place: 144 Moyser Road
A.R.P. Post: I.80

Photos taken in the back gardens of Moyser and Longstone Roads.

Some Local Reminiscences

Sydney Potter

I was a member of D Company of the Streatham Battalion of the Home Guard. Our headquarters were at 20 Leigham Court Road. The original function of the Home Guard was to assist in countering a possible German invasion. By 1944 the prospect of an invasion had receded, but there were fears of renewed air attacks possibly with secret weapons. To counter this threat new air defences were installed consisting of batteries of rocket launchers. There were 64 of these so-called "Z" launchers each firing two rockets simultaneously - a somewhat terrifying experience. The Home Guard were given special training to man these sites. Although there was a "Z" site on Tooting Common, D Company were transferred to a site in the grounds of an evacuated school at the foot of Anerley Hill. We slept in the school building but were called out to man the guns when there was an air raid alert.

I was paid ½d a mile to cycle to and from Anerley (rather derisory pay for cycling up Central Hill on the way out and Anerley Hill on the return journey.) One night in, I think, August 1944, a V-1 crashed and exploded on the site killing and maiming many of our Company. By a happy (for me) coincidence, I had taken a night's leave (to which I was entitled every four weeks) on this same night and so escaped the carnage. Nevertheless, a policeman knocked on our door in Mount Ephraim Road to report that I was missing following the incident.

Jim French

The French family lived at 53 Lanercost Road, between Christchurch and Palace Roads. There was Mum, myself (aged 13 and attending the South London Emergency Secondary School based at Alleyn's) and my brother David, aged five. Dad was in the Army, a minor cog in the Enigma-decoding operation at Bletchley Park. In one of our front rooms we had a Morrison shelter under which the family slept. It was a few weeks after the Doodlebug offensive was launched that Lanercost Road was hit. You could tell from the volume of the whining rocket engine noise at cut-out point when one was going to crash near you. We knew this one was going to be damn close. It was. It crashed in the next-door-but-two garden.

In that garden was an Anderson shelter and five or six people were killed there. In our room all the windows were blown in, but an extremely large wardrobe was toppled against the shelter, helping shield us from flying glass but not the smoke and fug. Brother David asked: "Mummy, are we dead?" - as good a tension-breaker as could be expected in the circumstances. Upstairs, in my first floor bedroom that I had quit a few weeks before, half the walls were blown in, and more than a hundred bricks were piled up on my bed. Even with my thick skin, I could not have survived that. Our house was 25-33% destroyed. It was eventually restored. No.51 was 67% destroyed and pulled down. Lambeth put up about 16 prefabs on the bomb site and, later, the tall flats and other dwellings that are there today.

The night we were bombed out we kipped down in the house of a policeman friend named Burton, at the bottom of Lanercost Road. My father returned on compassionate leave and the evening after the bomb, he took me to see *Gone With the Wind* at the Regal, Streatham.

Seeking rehousing, my mother joined a queue at Lambeth housing office in Acre Lane, Brixton. A council official said he was sorry they had run out of requisitioned houses for the time being but could possible help if anyone knew of an empty property. My mother had done her homework and advanced to tell the official about No.4 Gubyon Avenue, Herne Hill. We eventually moved in. But many of those other bombed-out people were reluctant to leave the queue for rehousing. Several of them were killed by another doodlebug soon after my mother had left to return home.

Daniel Currie

After our destroyer, H.M.S."Swift", was sunk on 24th June 1944, I was sent on survivor's leave. Then I was sent to London with many other sailors to help with their terrible difficulty. We were, in fact, on rescue and demolition. By Golly, it would have been safer at sea. We were doing work at Balham putting windows back which were blown out by blast - white parchment paper at the top and black at the bottom, making new temporary wooden frames. Also we put tiles back on roofs.

Then the doodlebugs would arrive, off the roofs we would get, dash to the gable end of the street (Cavendish Road), stand with our back flat to the wall, watch and wait. They came over maybe 6 or 7, pass overhead, *then* some of the blighters would turn back, the engine stops then they dive down.

We were stationed at South Kensington. We travelled by lorries to various areas to make things safe for people after the damage.

One thing I will never forget was later on we were coming from Croydon one Saturday lunch-time [25th November 1944] on the way to our depot. We just got to the lights before New Cross about 12 o'clock, when there was a flash and what a bang! Our lorry went up and down with a wallop; bloody noses, bit of a shock. It was a rocket hitting Woolworths a few hundred yards down the road. Just a large heap of brick were left when we got there. I think 84 dead [official count: more than 160 - Britain's worst V-2 attack].

We were there till one in the morning searching for people in some of the offices on the left. We dug with our hands for people. Some office girls were killed just by the blast. It would take me too long to tell of the gruesome things we found. We had rubber gloves and overalls - it was sickening. But in the quiet spells we really enjoyed helping these gritty determined Londoners who would not give in to that lot.

Bomb 30

Date: 21st July 1944
Time: evening
Place: 131 Hopton Road/Valley Road
A.R.P. Post: J.91

A second bomb of the day fell between Hopton and Valley Roads, opposite Hill House Road. The night was a wet one and thoroughly unpleasant for all concerned. Nearby wardens ran to the scene, and S.W. Bookless was quickly hard at it, although the house he lived in was wrecked beyond repair.

Damage had already been caused in the area by Bomb 25.

Most of the casualties were recovered quickly and sent away for treatment, but Mr George Garland of 131 Hopton Road proved very hard to find, and the rescue parties toiled by the light of flares for many hours before his body was ultimately recovered.

P.W. Jones acted as Incident Officer, setting up his post on the corner of Hill House Road. It was with somewhat mixed feelings that Mr Jones saw next day that the neighbouring house was labelled by the surveyor as "Dangerous Structure".

Owing to the split nature of the incident, D.D.Ws. Albert Sheppard and Edward Tinson decided that a second point of control was necessary and installed D.P.W.Ford, of J.89, in Hopton Road.

This map is based on the Ordnance Survey 60" map published in 1938

Bomb 31

Date: 22nd July 1944
Time: 6.10 a.m.
Place: Lutheran Place
A.R.P. Post: K.101

Bomb 31 dropped in Lutheran Place, among the compact zone of small cottages and stores built around 1860 at the top of Brixton Hill. There was much damage inflicted.

Masson Seeley's engineering factory had extensive damage.

Over the Lambeth border, many surrounding roads suffered slight damage but there were no casualties. The shop fronts along Upper Tulse Hill and Somers Place were shattered.

This area had already suffered a number of bombs during the Blitz.

A box factory destroyed belonged to the company of which Warden Wixcey was a director.

Nearby were the stables of the Co-op. milk distributing organisation, but the horses stood it very well, and there was little dislocation, thanks to quick action by the staff.

George and Daisy Sales, an elderly couple, of 19 Lutheran Place, were among the three fatalities. The total casualties were about a dozen.

A laundry destroyed belonged to P.W.Pumfrett of K.101. His manager was killed outright whilst keeping watch, his family being in the firm's shelter since they had been previously bombed out of their home. Notwithstanding this double loss, Mr Pumfrett took on the job of I.O. and discharged the responsibility commendably.

Twenty-three days after the incident a cat was recovered from one of the wrecked Lutheran cottages and there can be little doubt it was incarcerated for the whole of this period, without serious ill-effects.

BRIXTON HILL

COWPER'S ROW

BACK LANE

UPPER TULSE HILL

LUTHERAN PLACE

School

This map is based on the Ordnance Survey 60" map published in 1936

Bomb 32

Date: 23rd July 1944
Time: early a.m.
Place: St.Anselm's Church, Madeira Road.
A.R.P. Post: J.89

Post J.89 received the next flying bomb and it fell in the very early hours, near the half-demolished St.Anselm's Church. D.P.W.Ford was I.O., with his control point in Madeira Road, and P.W. Frankford looked after the damage in Oakdale Road, while D.D.Ws. Sheppard and Tinson were early on the scene. Quickly Rescue Parties and N.F.S. set to work on the wrecked houses in both roads.

Eugene Griffiths was killed when a H.E. bomb landed on 28 Madeira Road on 16th October 1940.

GLENELDON ROAD

MADEIRA ROAD

At 15 Madeira Road Francis Fox was killed.

In the later stages a small fire broke out in Oakdale Road and the many N.F.S. present appeared to compete for the honour of extinguishing it. During the operation quite a few people got rather wet.

St.Anselm's Church

St. Anselm's Church had suffered earlier blast damage but the V-1 rendered it unusable and it did not survive after the war.

OAKDALE ROAD

At 1 Oakdale Road an Anderson shelter had been erected indoors in the hall - unfortunately it was not on a solid floor, there being a cellar underneath. Searchers eventually managed to get into the cellar from another point and the rescue work proceeded from above and below simultaneously, but to no avail. The occupants, an elderly married couple and a parent, had been killed outright.

HOPTON ROAD

A bomb hit 73 Hopton Road in December 1940.

This was one of several incidents at which Dr Charles Grosch was present.

Farnan Hall was used by the Ministry of Food for a flour store.

This map is based on the Ordnance Survey 60" map published in 1935

Bomb 33

Date: 27th July 1944
Time: midnight
Place: Wavertree Road/Daysbrook Road
A.R.P. Post: K.100

Just before midnight a bomb fell at the junction of Daysbrook and Wavertree Roads, right opposite the Company H.Q. of the Home Guard and the Streatham High School for Girls, which both suffered severely. The incident was just in K.100 but K.99 post being nearer, they got there first, and P.W. Herbert Dando took charge as I.O.

Reservoir

Some exceptionally fine rescue work was performed, including the recovery at 12 Daysbrook Road of two trapped casualties from a Morrison shelter on which the whole house had collapsed. One of these two ladies, Mrs Cornelius Buysman, wrote a letter of thanks from the Guildford Hospital where she was recovering to the rescue services. This is reproduced opposite.

DAYSBROOK ROAD

Charles Kerbey was killed at 23 Wavertree Road.

WAVERTREE ROAD

An innovation at this incident was the loud-speaker kindly supplied by Tannoy Ltd., which D.P.W.Lean of K.100 had fixed to the car of the S.D.W. earlier in the evening, saying, "I hope we don't see you up in our area with it." It proved very useful.

The Streatham Hill High School was badly damaged by the blast. Some of the pupils were evacuated to Halifax, but by the beginning of the new term temporary premises were secured in Herne Hill and the school soldiered on. The old hall was enlarged and the new building was re-opened on 22nd October 1952 by H.R.H. The Duchess of Gloucester. A plaque commemorates the bombing.

Eustace Belham, "K" D.D.W., and the W.V.S. cared for the bombed-out victims in the school until coaches took them to the Rest Centre. The Home Guard under Major Remnant, were present in strength and helped a lot.

This map is based on the Ordnance Survey 60" map published in 1936

Bomb 33

Date: 27th July 1944
Time: midnight
Place: Wavertree Road/Daysbrook Road
A.R.P. Post: K.100

There were five of us in the building: the caretakers who lived in the School, and generally slept in the big cupboard under the front stone staircase, Mrs Dixon, the secretary who had come to live in School because her own flat was damaged, Miss James and I. The siren was late that night and I strolled through the empty dining room into the little shelter at the end, where we put up our camp beds. We both settled down to read, ears cocked. Soon in the distance the faint sound of the flying bomb drew nearer and nearer - yes, it was coming along "our lane". It had stopped - the deadly silence. "This is ours," I said. "Put your head under the pillow," said Miss James. I sat up to hear better, paralysed into stillness. The whirr of its horrible wings were over the roof - we heard them - was it our last moment? By a miracle it had cleared the roof of the Gymnasium and in its last downward plunge had fallen between the School and the house on the other side of Wavertree Road (in their garden, in fact). I have never heard so tremendous a noise, a noise compounded of so many noises, falling glass, splitting timber, crashing bricks and masonry, water pouring from burst pipes, doors and window frames hurling themselves through empty rooms - all individual noises and yet enveloping us in one great violent assault. An uncanny silence followed broken only by the dripping of water in the Dining Room next door.

M. Jarrett
Streatham Hill & Clapham High School Magazine, 1945

Warren Road Hospital, Guildford.
Dear Sir,

I would like to express my grateful thanks to the Civil Defence workers who rescued my friend and myself when the house was totally demolished by a direct hit. All the services seemed to arrive within a few minutes. Your marvellous and humane C.D. workers had found us under that mass of debris within an hour and by their skill and bravery had us out of that wonderful invention, the Morrison Table, in a few minutes. Would you convey to these men our very grateful thanks for saving our lives and to the doctors for the valuable services, so generously given after a long day's work.

I should also like to include the W.V.S., who so kindly prepared hot drinks for us and stood by, in spite of the great danger, during the night and welcomed us on our return from "the grave".

The ambulance driver and nurse soon had us at South London Hospital and I do thank them most sincerely for their help in face of great risk.

The hospital people were splendid and gave us great comfort and most kindly treatment till they sent us here on 29th. I cannot sufficiently express my thanks and admiration for all who helped and for the splendid administration and co-operation of the Streatham Civil Defence. You are a marvellous body of men and women.

Yours gratefully,
H.C.A.Buysman

Daysbrook Road the day after the Bomb.

Bomb 34

Date: 1st August 1944
Time: 7 a.m.
Place: 150 Leigham Court Road
A.R.P. Post: K.92

Post K.92 had its third fly bomb, round about breakfast time - as usual for them. Some big houses in Leigham Court Road were badly hit, but the bulk of the damage was on the other side of the road in the Borough of Lambeth. The Government-encouraged policy of evacuation proved its value at this incident, for although normally there were eleven persons living in the worst-damaged house, all had gone away but one, and he had spent the night with a neighbour. Useful confirmation of this happy situation was secured from the milk roundsman.

Two bay windows of 93 Palace Road, ½ mile to the north, crashed to the ground.

Most of the damage was inflicted on the Lambeth side. Severe blast affected Leigham Court Road, Glennie Road and St. Peter's Church. Two minor casualties were sent to a First Aid Post. By noon, road clearing was being done and 50 pioneers and 30 Naval ratings were repairing homes.

People standing in a bus queue and several passers-by flung themselves to the gound as the bomb roared overhead.

152 Leigham Court Road, the home of the late Stanley Lupino, was badly damaged.

The casualties were three minor ones, and the incident was closed in a very short time. S.W. William Morley again acted as I.O. in a satisfactory manner.

St. Peter's Church, built in 1871, was badly damaged. All the stained glass windows were blown in, the roofing stripped off and the conical turret on the west front crashed to the ground.

This map is based on the Ordnance Survey 60" map published in 1936

Bomb 35

Date: 3rd August 1944
Time: 3 a.m.
Place: Pendle Road
A.R.P. Post: I.77

The bomb fell about 3 a.m. at the rear of houses in Pendle Road, bringing down several, and involved some Anderson shelters from which a number of casualties were recovered. With twelve dead, this was the most serious of Streatham's 41 incidents.

D.D.W. Walter Ames acted as Incident Officer through the night, with Miss Enniss as clerk, handing over to his co-deputy, William Dineen. Mr Dineen was relieved in turn by D.P.W. Curtis, who held the fort all through the next day, during which rescue operations proceeded - the last body not being recovered until 5 p.m.

An example of the marvellous spirit of the bombed-out occurred at the Streatham mobile canteen during the night, when an elderly lady in night attire and overcoat, with an eiderdown draped over her shoulders, came along for a cup of tea. As she drank it and munched a sandwich she said, "Dear me, if I'd known I was going to a tea-party I'd have put my best frock on." The laugh she got was very near to tears.

Alf Ford, aged 72, of 117 Pendle Road was killed. His wife had recently died after an illness, and he had just retired after 33 years with the Streatham Sorting Office. He was a pigeon fancier, and many of his birds were working in the pigeon post.

This was a tragic incident for P.W.Woods, of Post I.78, for one of the fatal casualties was his sister-in-law.

Five women - possibly French or Belgian refugees - were killed at number 121.

A novel feature was the assistance given to the Rescue parties by naval personnel who had been working in the area on first-aid repairs to damage caused by earlier bombs.

Albert Dorrell, of 122 Pretoria Road, a member of the Home Guard, died later in St.James Hospital.

Four bombs were dropped along a flight killing two women at 88 Pendle Road on 3rd October 1940.

One task the W.V.S. undertook was to find a good home for the lovely pedigree Scotch terrier, which the bombed-out owners could not take with them to their evacuation address.

The loud-speaker on the warden's car proved invaluable in securing information from the bystanders and neighbours, verifying the house cards (which were carefully checked by Messrs. Walsh and Archer) and quickly resolving many of the rumours which inevitably float around any long incident. Mention should also be made of the two Randalls - C.D. messengers who gave splendid service for many hours.

A H.E. bomb fell on 15th September 1940.

During the afternoon Lady Reading, chairman of the W.V.S., visited the Incident Inquiry Point, which was in charge of Mrs Fisher, I.77 Post Leader.

PENDLE ROAD

PRETORIA ROAD

WELHAM ROAD

This map is based on the Ordnance Survey 60" map published in 1935

Bomb 36

Date: 3rd August 1944
Time:
Place: 14 Abbotsleigh Road
A.R.P. Post: I.81

ULLATHORNE ROAD

ABBOTSLEIGH ROAD

ALDRINGTON ROAD

Whilst the incident in Pendle Road was still proceeding, another fly bomb fell in Post I.81 at Abbotsleigh Road.

This was the first incident that the mobile team went into action. It had been set up to handle the times when most wardens were at work. D.P.W.Harrison was I.O., D.P.W.Rippon was the clerk, Mr White was loading ground warden and Mr Moore was the runner. One must not forget to mention the warden of Post I.78, who proudly claimed he just managed to beat the mobile team to the incident.

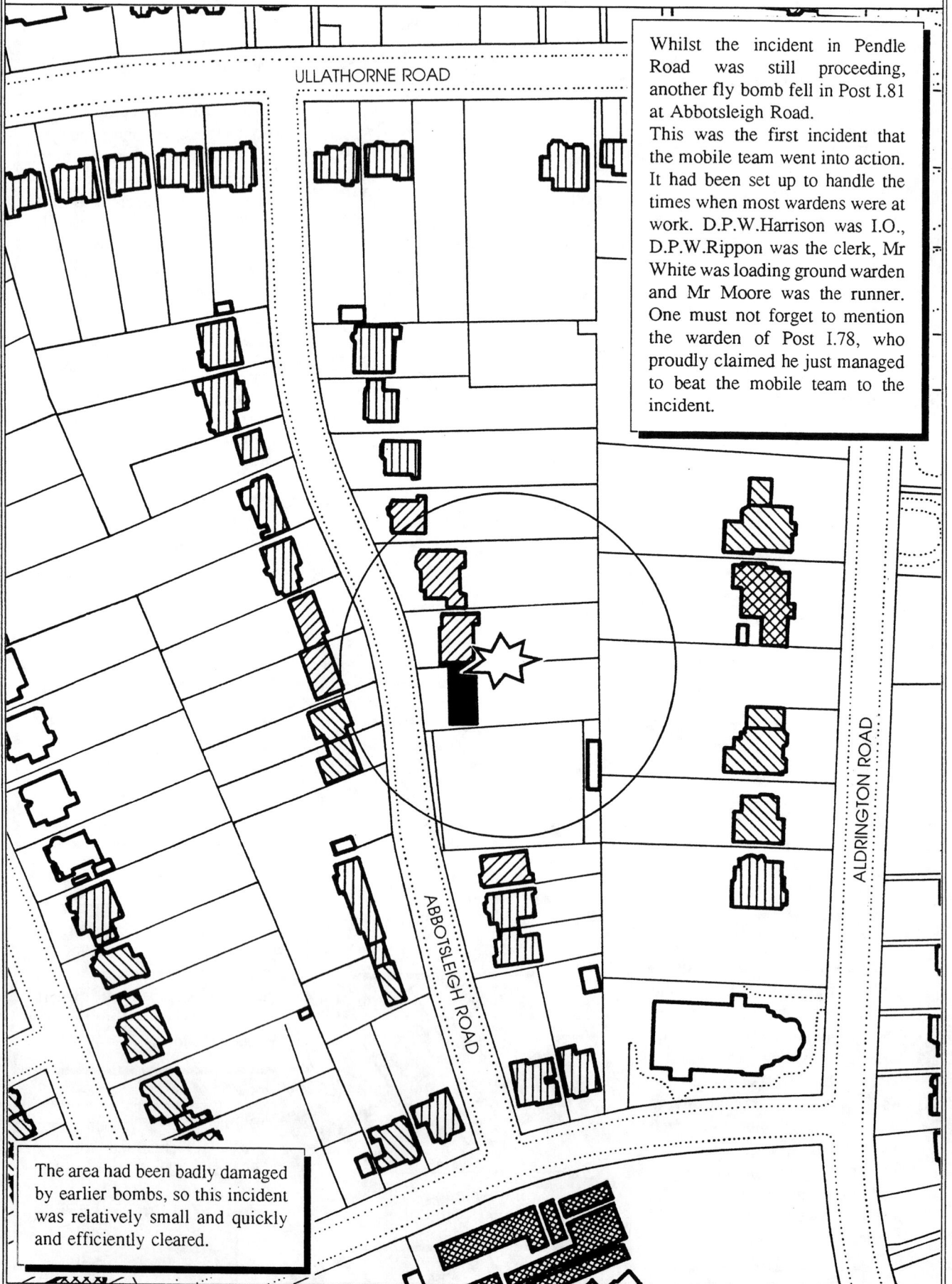

The area had been badly damaged by earlier bombs, so this incident was relatively small and quickly and efficiently cleared.

This map is based on the Ordnance Survey 60" maps published in 1936 and 1938

Bomb 37

Date: 5th August 1944
Time: early a.m.
Place: Moyser Road
A.R.P. Post: I.80

The third bomb in succession to fall in "I" district arrived before dawn, and chose the border of I.80, so that I.77 and I.81 were also affected.

D.D.W. Walter Ames acted as I.O., with P.W. Fred Archer, of I.81, as assistant; Warden Alexander was clerk and Warden Weston occupants' checker. This job proved rather troublesome and over half an hour after the bomb fell there were 30 persons unaccounted for, although it seemed certain nothing like that number were still trapped. The loud-speaker proved its worth, for within ten minutes of the announcement asking for all available information to be given to the I.O., the list of 30 missing had been reduced to two.

In Pretoria Road, which was badly knocked about, one householder was carefully sweeping the broken tiles and glass from his gateway, although it looked as if the whole house might collapse any moment. "What gets me wild," he confided to a passing warden, "is that I've just paid my ruddy rates in advance!"

The Rescue services distinguished themselves, and made another splendid recovery from a Morrison shelter in the heart of a wrecked house.

Fire Guard Frank Corben died at his home at Number 36 Moyser Road. He had lived in Streatham for nearly 25 years. Two years later his wife, Lilian, wrote: "The days go by but loneliness and heartache still remain."

Alice Ramson died at 30 Moyser Road.

There was a large crater with burst gas and water mains in Moyser Road near the junction with Pretoria Road and property was damaged over a wide area.

The Borough Controller visited the incident and laid emphasis on the need for full after-raid services. It was, therefore, sheer cussedness that the Ministry of Food canteen ordered to supply breakfast to the bombed-out reported to Moyser Road, *Wanstead*, instead of *Wandsworth*. Later in the day mobile canteens and other facilities were made available and much appreciated.

There were two fatal casualties, and ten were taken to hospital. Permission to close the incident was granted within three hours of the bomb falling - quick work having regard to the circumstances. Wardens specially commended by the I.O. included Messrs. Greenhalgh, Harris, Hartland, Habberfield, Raybaud, and Misses Hill and Murray. The two messengers, Randall and Letchford, were especially useful.

PRETORIA ROAD

MOYSER ROAD

PENWORTHAM ROAD

This map is based on the Ordnance Survey 60" map published in 1936

Bomb 38

Date: 6th August 1944
Time:
Place: Aldrington Road
A.R.P. Post: I.81

Streatham Park continued its ill-luck when a bomb landed in Aldrington Road at the junction with Ullathorne Road. P.W. Fred Archer of I.81 took over as I.O., with Senior Fire Guard Watkins as clerk.

A large gas main was set alight and a big tree had been almost uprooted. Both these dangers were dealt with by the ever-resourceful N.F.S. Military personnel placed at the disposal of the I.O. were used to control traffic and the Fire Guard Sector Captain gave very useful information for the check-up of occupants in the damaged houses.

The only casualty was a passer-by, who was quickly despatched to hospital.

ULLATHORNE ROAD

ALDRINGTON ROAD

The area to the south had already been devastated by flying bombs 17 and 36.

The total time of this incident from bomb-fall to official closure was just forty minutes - surely a record for speed.

This map is based on the Ordnance Survey 60" maps published in 1936 and 1938

Bomb 38

Date: 6th August 1944
Time:
Place: Aldrington Road
A.R.P. Post: I.81

Photographs taken in Streatham Park in May 1947 showing ruined houses - probably those in Aldrington Road.

Bomb 39

Date: 9th August 1944
Time: 6.45 a.m.
Place: Tierney Road
A.R.P. Post: K.99

The fly bomb fell in Tierney Road bringing down five big houses and damaging a large amount of surrounding property. Post Warden Herbert Dando was I.O., well supported by wardens of K.99 and neighbouring posts.

160 of Dumbarton Court's 230 flats were reported damaged by the blast.

Streatham Place was then narrower than today, but it proved possible to operate this incident and yet permit normal traffic, including buses, to use the road. This was due to close co-operation between the police and C.D. Services. The troops of a military convoy which went by seemed to be extremely interested in the damage caused.

Knights printing works had damage to the roof and valuable machinery was exposed to the weather. Most concern was for food stores but Preece the grocers and Brown the bakers were the only ones damaged by the blast. Marshall's factory in Morrish Road was practically unharmed.

Streatham Place had its fair share of bombs during the Blitz.

Towards the close of the incident a fire broke out in the wreckage of one house, probably due to an electrical short. The N.F.S. were recalled and quickly dealt with it.

Casualties occurred in Tierney Road, Streatham Place and also Montrell, Sulina and Christchurch Roads. About eight went to hospital and twenty to F.A.P.5.

This map is based on the Ordnance Survey 60" map published in 1936

Bomb 40

Date: 13th August 1944
Time: a.m.
Place: 3 Bellasis Avenue
A.R.P. Post: K.97

Fifteen casualties were sent to hospital and rather less to First Aid Post No.5. Fortunately, there were no fatalities.

Streatham's last two bombs fell within 15 minutes of each other, early one Sunday morning. The first of these gave K.97 its fifth, which thus achieved the uneviable highest record for any Streatham Post. The bomb fell between houses in Bellasis and Thornton Avenues, and caused much damage in both these and other nearby roads.

Warden Henry Steele acted as I.O. in a very satisfactory manner.

A delayed action bomb fell on Telford Park Tennis Club on 17th October 1940.

A H.E. bomb was dropped on 97 Sternhold Avenue on a run over Streatham on 12th November 1940.

A delayed action bomb fell on 32 Sternhold Avenue on 10th September 1940.

D.P.W. Jens Hansen of 91 Sternhold was injured by debris from the explosion but persisted in carrying on. At one stage he was persuaded to get into an ambulance but before it moved off he was out again and quite late in the afternoon was still about the scene of the incident with a bandage round his head.

During the day the Mayor of Wandsworth (Alderman Bonney) visited this incident and No.41 in "I" District, accompanied by the Chief Warden (Alderman Evan Rees). He talked with many of those whose homes had been damaged and congratulated the wardens on doing a good job.

This map is based on the Ordnance Survey 60" maps published in 1935 and 1936

Bomb 41

Date: 13th August 1944
Time: a.m.
Place: 132/134 Crowborough Road
A.R.P. Post: I.79

The last fly bomb on Streatham fell at the junction of Crowborough and Ramsdale Roads. The bomb fell on the rear gardens in the midst of a cluster of Anderson shelters, and the degree of protection afforded was amazing. It was undoubtedly due to this, plus the amount of evacuation which had taken place, that the number of casualties was so low. There were no trapped casualties at all, nor were there any fatalities.

These houses were hit twice in 1940 during the Blitz.

P.W. Fred Greetham, although on the sick list, took charge of the incident at the start, and when D.D.W. Ames took over, carried on very pluckily as his assistant.

The W.V.S. opened an Incident Information Post in the pavilion of Furzedown College, which was the nearest suitable place.

A considerable number of Tooting Home Guards worked both in the morning and afternoon helping to tidy up houses, move furniture and deal with first-aid repairs. In the latter connection supplies of materials were immediately made available at I.80 warden's stand-by post - the issue being announced over the loud-speaker. A Salvation Army Canteen supplying soup at mid-day was similarly made known. Furniture removals and first-aid repairs also went forward under borough auspices, getting into action with commendable speed. At a later stage both the mobile baths and laundry attended.

Great damage was done in Gorse Rise and other roads in the neighbourhood.

For once, it was a lovely sunny morning and whether this had anything to do with it or not, the standard of public morale was really exceptional. Being Sunday, nearly everybody was at home and the thirsty work of clearing up brought a constant stream to the Streatham Mobile Canteen. Three times were supplies replenished and the staff were 'flat out' for nearly four hours.

This map is based on the Ordnance Survey 60" map published in 1936